H. C Clarke, Thomas P Ashmore

The Confederate States Almanac, and Repository of Useful Knowledge, for 1863

Being the third Year of the Independence of the Confederate States of America. Vol. I

H. C Clarke, Thomas P Ashmore

The Confederate States Almanac, and Repository of Useful Knowledge, for 1863
Being the third Year of the Independence of the Confederate States of America. Vol. I

ISBN/EAN: 9783337248239

Printed in Europe, USA, Canada, Australia, Japan

Cover: Foto ©ninafisch / pixelio.de

More available books at **www.hansebooks.com**

CONFEDERATE STATES

ALMANAC,

AND

REPOSITORY OF USEFUL KNOWLEDGE,

FOR THE YEAR

1863.

H. C. CLARKE,
VICKSBURG, MISS.

Entered according to Act of Congress, in the year 1861, by

H. C. CLARKE,

In the Clerk's office of the District Court of the Confederate States for the District of Mississippi.

PREFACE.

The second volume of the Confederate States Almanac is now offered to the people of the South. The publisher is perfecting arrangements that will insure the permanent issue of the work every year. The leading object of the publication will be to make it the repository of the largest possible amount of useful information, embracing every variety of knowledge. Annual statistics from all the States in the Confederacy, showing the progress in Population, Manufactures, Commerce, Wealth and all the elements of prosperity. The contents of this volume is not altogether perfect, or full, in some details of statistics.

Owing to the state of affairs in the country, the compiler found it impossible to obtain full Reports from all the States. Of the information contained in this volume, great pains has been taken to make them as accurate as possible from the resources at hand. The Reports of the Departments of the Confederate Government have been taken from the latest official documents, and will be found interesting.

The financial resources of individual States were taken from the last Reports. Much valuable information has been compiled from the United States census of 1860, which will be found exceedingly interesting at the present time.

The Astronomical calculations, &c., have been prepared by Thomas P. Ashmore, of Georgia. The calculations will be found full and accurate. In a work like this, designed to embrace so much variety of matter, there is no doubt some errors. The compiler would be under obligations to the patrons of the work for any valuable hints, communications or correction of errors, or improvements in the Almanac. Address the publisher.

VICKSBURG, MISS.

1863   1863

THE

Confederate States

ALMANAC,

AND

REPOSITORY OF USEFUL KNOWLEDGE,

FOR 1863.

Being the Third Year of the Independence of the Confederate States of America.

AUGUSTA, GA.,   VICKSBURG, MISS.,

H. C. CLARKE,

PUBLISHER,

1863.

Vol. 2nd.   1st Series.

SIGNS OF THE ZODIAC AND INFLUENCE OF THE MOON

The Moon is supposed by some to have a special influence upon different parts of the bodies of men and animals, as it passes through the signs of the Zodiac. The following cut is inserted for the sake of those who believe in this imaginary influence, and is intended to represent the part of the body affected by the Moon when it is in any particular sign of the Zodiac. By finding the Moon's place in the proper column of the calendar pages, and comparing it with this cut, the particular part which is supposed to be affected, will be at once seen. Thus, when the Moon is in Aries (♈), it is supposed to influence the head and face; when in Capricornus (♑) the knees, etc.

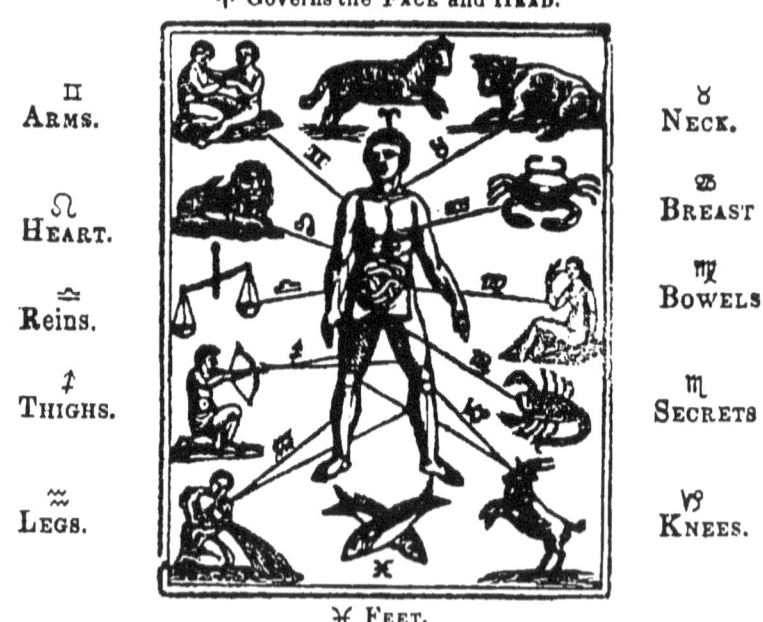

♈ Governs the FACE and HEAD.

♊ ARMS.

♌ HEART.

♎ Reins.

♐ THIGHS.

♒ LEGS.

♉ NECK.

♋ BREAST.

♍ BOWELS.

♏ SECRETS.

♑ KNEES.

♓ FEET.

NAMES AND CHARACTERS OF THE SIGNS OF THE ZODIAC.

♈ Aries, the Ram. ♉ Taurus, the Bull. ♊ Gemini, the Twins. ♋ Cancer, the Crab. ♌ Leo, the Lion. ♍ Virgo, the Virgin. ♎ Libra, the Balance. ♏ Scorpio, the Scorpion. ♐ Sagittarius, the Archer. ♑ Capricornus, the Goat. ♒ Aquarius, the Waterman. ♓ Pisces, the Fishes.

CHRONOLOGICAL CYCLES.

Dominical Letter,	D.	Solar Cycle,	24
Golden Number,	2	Roman Indiction,	6
Epact, (Moon's age,) Jan. 1st	11	Julian Period	6576

MOVEABLE FEASTS OF THE CHURCH.

Septuagesima Sunday,	Feb. 1	Rogation Sunday,	May 10
Quin. or Shrove Sunday,	Feb. 15	Ascension Day,	May 14
Ash-Wednesday,	Feb. 18	Whit-Sunday,	May 24
Palm Sunday,	Mar. 29	Advent Sunday	Nov 29
Easter Sunday.	April 5		

ECLIPSES FOR 1863.

THE first will be of the Sun, on the 17th of May, at 11h. 15m. A. M., invisible in America.

The second will be a total Eclipse of the Moon, on the 1st day of June, partially visible, and is calculated to apparent time, as follows:

	DAY.	H'R.	MIN.	SEC.
The Eclipse begins on June	1,	4	17	38.
Beginning of total darkness	"	5	24	36.
End of total darkness	"	6	31	18.
The Moon will rise at Augusta with 7 2-10 digits eclipsed on her Western limb.	"	7	1	0,
The Eclipse will end	"	7	38	16.
Duration of visibility	"	0	37	16.

(P. M.)

The third will be of the Sun, on the 11th of Nov., at 2h. 36m. A. M., invisible in America.

The fourth will be of the Moon, on the 25th day of November, visible and nearly total throughout the continent of America, and is calculated to apparent time, as follows:

	DAY.	H'R.	MIN.	SEC.
Beginning at Augusta, Ga.,	Nov. 25	1	57	14.
Middle of Eclipse	"	3	37	53.
Ecliptic Opposition	"	3	43	21.
End of Eclipse	"	5	18	32.
Duration	"	3	21	18.

(A. M.)

Digits eclipsed 11 1-2, on the Moon's north limb.

At the greatest obscuration, about 1-24 part of the Moon's diameter, will remain uneclipsed.

EQUINOXES AND SOLSTICES.

Vernal Equinox, ...(Spring begins)..............March 21st.
Summer Solstice,............(Summer begins)............June 21st.
Autumnal Equinox,.........(Autumn begins).............Sept. 23d.
Winter Solstice,............(Winter begins)..............Dec. 21st.

ASPECTS OF THE PLANETS.

The Planet Venus will be Evening Star till September 29th, then Morning Star till the end of the year.

Jupiter will be in opposition with the Sun, on the 12th of April, when he will shine with his greatest brilliancy.

Saturn will be in opposition with the Sun, on the 20th of March, when he will be brightest.

Mars will be too near the Sun to afford any favorable opportunity of viewing him this year.

THE TWELVE SIGNS OF THE ZODIAC.

Spring Signs,........ 1. ♓ Pisces. 2. ♈ Aries.   3. ♉ Taurus
Summer Signs,....... 4. ♊ Geminii 5. ♋ Cancer. 6. ♌ Leo.
Autumn Signs. ..... 7. ♍ Virgo.   8. ♎ Libra.   9. ♏ Scorpio,
Winter Signs, ...10. ♐ Sagitt'us 11. ♑ Capri'us. 12. ♒ Aquarius.

The first six are called Northern Signs, and the other six Southern Signs

TABLE OF THE PRINCIPAL BODIES IN THE SOLAR SYSTEM.

NAMES.	Mean Diameter.	Mean Distance from the Sun.	Revolution ar'd the Sun.	Revolution on Axis.	Velocity per m. in orbit.	Size—the Earth being 1.	Density.— Earth b'ng 1	Light, Earth b'ng 1
	Miles.	Miles.	yrs. days	d. h. M.	Miles.			
The Sun..	883,246	....	25	9 59	....	1,412,921,101	0.252	Infin-
Mercury..	3,224	36,814,000	88	1 0 5	1,827	0,053	1.120	6.680
Venus	7,687	68,787,000	224	.. 23 21	1,338	0,909	0.923	1.911
The Earth	7,912	95,103,000	1	.. 23 56	1,138	1,000	1.000	1.000
The Moon	2,180	95,103,000	1 ...	27 7 43	38	0,020	0.615	1.000
Mars	4,189	144,908,000	1 321	1 0 37	921	0,125	0.948	0.431
Jupiter ...	80,170	494,797,000	11 215	.. 9 56	496	1,456,000	0 238	0,037
Saturn ...	79,042	907,168,000	29 167	.. 10 29	368	771,000	0.138	0.011
Uranus...	35,112	1,824,290,000	84 6	1 13 33	259	89,000	0.242	0,003
Neptune..	41,500	2,854,099,000	164 226	.. .. ..	208	143,000	0,140	0.001

NOTE.---There are more than fifty small Planets or Asteroids, between the orbit of Mars and Jupiter.

MEAN AND APPARENT TIME.

MEAN TIME is the time indicated by a well-regulated clock or watch running without variation, so as to make the day, or 24 hours, equal to the Mean Time at which the Sun comes to the meridian during the year. Apparent Time is the time which makes the Sun come to the meridian every day at 12 o'clock. On account of the elipticity of the earth's orbit, and its inclination to the equator, the sun does not always come to the meridian in exactly the same time; and hence, Apparent Time is irregular, and either gradually falls behind Mean Time, or gains on it, sometimes to the amount of more than sixteen minutes. When the Sun comes to the meridian earlier than the Mean Time, it is said to be fast; but when it comes to it later, it is said to be slow; and the amount by which Apparent Time differs from Mean Time is called the Equation of Time. In order to set a timepiece according to Mean Time, it is necessary to have a dial, or noon mark; and allowance must be made for the Equation of Time. This Almanac is in Mean Time.

EXPLANATION OF THE SIGNS USED IN THIS ALMANAC.

● New Moon, and Moon generally, ☽ First Quarter, ☉ Full Moon, ☾ Last Quarter ☊ Moon's ascending node, or dragon's head. ☋ Moon's descending node, or dragon's tail. IN APOGEE—Moon farthest from the Earth IN PERIGEE- Moon nearest the earth. ● Highest—Moon far thest North ● Lowest -Moon farthest South. ♄ Saturn. ♀ Venus ☌ near together. ♃ Jupiter. ☿ Mercury ☐ 90 deg. apart. ☍ Opposition or 180 degrees apart ♂ Mars. 7* Stars. ☼ Sun. ♅ Herschel.

Complete Court Calendars, &c. for the States of Alabama and Tennessee, will be inserted in orders of 10 gross and upwards from dealers ordering for circulation in those states respectively.

NOTE. Any person solving ten of the Problems contained in this Almanac, and sending to me at Americus, Ga., by the 15th of May next, the correct answers to the same, shall have the same acknowledged in the Almanac for 1864

A few original problems for 1864, are solicited. They must be thoroughly solved and explained, in order to meet with attention

T. P. ASHMORE.

1st Month,]   **JANUARY, 1863.**   **[31 Days]**

MOON'S PHASES.

	D.	H.	M.	
Full Moon,	4	9	46	eve.
Last Quarter	12	1	43	eve.
New Moon,	19	9	54	mo.
First Quarter,	26	3	45	eve.

PROBLEMS.

1. What must be the diameter of a balloon, in order that it may ascend with four persons, weighing each 160 pounds, and the balloon and bag of sand weighing 60 pounds.

D. of M.	D. of W.	Various Phenomena.	Sun rises H.M.	Sun sets H.M.	Moon's Place	Moon ri &sts H. M.	High tide Savannah H. M.
1	Thur	New Year's Day. Cold	7 44	5 56	♊	4 5	5 55
2	Frid	☉ in Perigee and	7 34	5 57		5 0	7 10
3	Satur	☾ highest chilly weather	7 34	5 57	♋	5 50	8 8
4	S.	Princeton Battle, 1777.	7 34	5 57		rises.	9 0
5	Mon	Cloudy and	7 24	5 58	♌	6 15	9 45
6	Tues	Epiphany. cold.	7 24	5 58		7 8	10 26
7	Wed		7 24	5 58	♍	8 20	11 2
8	Thur	Bat. N. Orleans, 1815.	7 14	5 59		9 13	11 38
9	Frid	Fair and frosty.	7 14	5 59		10 18	E. 14
10	Satur	Aldebaran sou 9h 8m.	7 05	6 0	♎	11 25	0 47
11	S.	Ala. & Fla. seced., '61.	7 05	6 0		morn.	1 24
12	Mon	Now more pleasant.	6 59	6 1	♏	0 30	2 2
13	Tues	Richard II. killed, 1490.	6 59	6 1		1 40	2 46
14	Wed	N. E. Winds	6 58	6 2	♐	2 50	3 47
15	Thur	and many	6 58	6 2		3 46	5 0
16	Frid	☾ lowest dark	6 57	6 3	♑	4 46	6 21
17	Satur	Bat. Cowpens, 1781.	6 57	6 3		5 30	7 30
18	S.	flying clouds.	6 56	6 4		6 31	8 16
19	Mon	Capella sou. 9h. 11m.	6 55	6 5	♒	sets.	9 2
20	Tues	☉ enters ♒ Geo sec '61,	6 55	6 5		6 30	9 45
21	Wed	High winds from	6 54	6 5	♓	7 34	10 25
22	Thur	Rigel sou. 8h- 48m.	6 54	6 6		8 35	11 5
23	Frid	N. W. and cold.	6 53	6 7		9 31	11 45
24	Satur	Augusta arsenal tak '61	6 52	6 7	♈	10 10	Morn.
25	S.	Cold and	6 51	6 9		11 8	0 28
26	Mon	Sirius sou. 10h. 1·m.	6 51	6 10	♉	morn.	1 18
27	Tues	Cloudy.	6 50	6 10		0 7	1 59
28	Wed	Perhaps snow	6 49	6 11	♊	1 8	2 57
29	Thur	Prof F. C. Bond died 59.	6 48	6 12		2 2	4 9
30	Frid	☾ highest.	6 48	6 12	♋	2 56	5 34
31	Satur	or sleet.	6 47	6 13		3 40	6 52

[2d Month.] FEBRUARY, 1863. [28 Days.

MOON'S PHASES.

	D.	H.	M
Full Moon	3	4	39 eve.
Last Quarter	11	1	51 mo.
New Moon	17	9	30 eve.
First Quarter	25	9	16 mo.

2. If the mercury in a barometer, at the bottom of a tower, be observed to stand at 30 inches, and, on being carried to the top of it, be observed 29.9 inches, what is the height of the tower?

3. Suppose a piece of marble contains 8 cubic feet, and weighs 1,353½ lbs., what is the specific gravity?

D. of M	D. of W	Various Phenomena.	Sun rises H. M.	Sun sets H. M.	MOON'S PLACE	Moon ri. st. H. M.	High tide Savannah. H. M.
1	S.	Septuagesima S.	6 46	5 14	♌	4 20	8 1
2	Mon.	Purification B. V. Mary.	6 45	5 15		5 15	8 49
3	Tue.	Fair and frosty.	6 44	5 16	♍	5 47	9 32
4	Wed.	[1780	6 44	5 16		rises.	10 9
5	Thu.	Earthquake at Sicily,	6 43	5 17	♎	8 30	10 43
6	Fri.	Damp and	6 42	5 18		9 14	11 14
7	Satu.	Sirius sou. 9h. 25m.	6 41	5 19	♏	10 25	11 46
8	S.	cloudy weather.	6 40	5 20		11 0	E 15
9	Mon.		6 39	5 21	♐	11 30	0 49
10	Tue.	Pro. Gov. Con. Stat.'61.	6 38	5 22		11 59	1 24
11	Wed.	Revolution in Domingo,	6 37	5 23		morn.	2 4
12	Thu.	☾ lowest. [1807.	6 36	5 24	♑	0 36	2 53
13	Fri.	Wind and	6 36	5 24		1 48	4 8
14	Sat.	Valentines cold.	6 35	5 25	♒	2 43	5 29
15	S.	Quinquag. Sun.	6 34	5 26		3 36	6 47
16	Mon.	Melancthon born, 1497.	6 33	5 27		4 50	7 52
17	Tue.	Sirius souths 8h. 50m.	6 32	5 28	♓	sets.	8 37
18	Wed.	Ash Wednesday.	6 31	5 29		7 30	9 22
19	Thu.	Sun enters ♓	6 30	5 30	♈	8 41	10 2
20	Fri	Much cloudy.	6 29	5 31		9 39	10 44
21	Sat.	weather and	6 28	5 32		10 25	11 27
22	S.	Washington born, 1732.	6 27	5 33	♉	10 49	morn.
23	Mon.	some rain.	6 26	5 34		11 20	0 16
24	Tue.	St. Mathias.	6 25	5 35	♊	11 58	0 54
25	Wed.	Now more pleasant.	6 24	5 36		morn.	1 41
26	Thu.	☾ highest.	6 23	5 37	♋	0 56	2 36
27	Frid.	Procyon south 9h. 3m.	6 22	5 38		1 47	3 49
28	Satu.	at the end of this month.	6 21	5 39	♌	2 36	5 16

3d Month,] **MARCH, 1863.** [31 Days.

MOON'S PHASES.

	D.	H.	M.	
Full Moon	5	9	21	mo
Last Quarter	12	0	15	eve
New Moon	19	9	17	mo
First Quarter	27	3	14	mo

4. The diameter of a balloon is 2,665 feet, what weight is it capable of raiisng?

5. What is the solidity in inches of several fragments or clear glass, whose weight is 13 ounces?

D. of M	D of W	Various Phenomena.	Sun rises H.	Sun rises M.	Sun sets H.	Sun sets M.	Moon's Place.	Moon ri. & sts H.	Moon ri. & sts M.	High tide Savan'ah H.	High tide Savan'ah M.
1	*S.*	St. David.	6	20	5	40		3	35	6	40
2	Mon	Procyon Sou. 9 h. 48 m.	6	19	5	41	♍	4	6	7	43
3	Tues	*Fair and frosty.*	6	18	5	42		4	44	8	29
4	Wed	Pollux Sou. 8 h. 44 m.	6	17	5	43	♎	5	19	9	10
5	Thur	La Place died, 1827.	6	16	5	44		rises.		9	43
6	Frid	*Cloudy and damp.*	6	15	5	45	♏	7	7	10	17
7	Satur	Regulus Sou. 10 h. 56 m.	6	14	5	46		8	0	10	46
8	*S.*	*Cold winds.*	6	13	5	47		8	53	11	17
9	Mon	Regulus Sou. 10 h. 48m.	6	12	5	48	♐	9	45	11	48
10	Tues	*from the N. W.*	6	11	5	49		10	37	Ev.	18
11	Wed	☽ lowest.	6	10	5	50	♑	11	29	0	59
12	Thur		6	9	5	51		morn.		1	30
13	Frid	♅ discovered 1781.	6	8	5	52	♒	0	20	2	19
14	Satur	*More mild.*	6	7	5	53		1	10	3	24
15	*S*	Jackson born, 1767.	6	6	5	54		1	57	4	51
16	Mon	Regulus sou. 10 h. 21m.	6	5	5	55	♓	2	43	6	11
17	Tues	St. Patrick.	6	4	5	56		3	27	7	18
18	Wed	*Stormy and*	6	3	5	57	♈	4	9	8	8
19	Thur	*unpleasant weather.*	6	2	5	58		sets.		8	58
20	Frid	♄ ☍ ☉ ♄ rises 5 h. 59 m.	6	1	5	59		7	40	9	35
21	Satur	Days and nights equal.	6	0	6	0	♉	8	35	10	21
22	*S.*	*Fair and more*	5	59	6	1		9	0	11	4
23	Mon	Regulus sou. 9h. 58 m.	5	58	6	2	♊	10	0	11	51
24	Tues	*pleasant.*	5	57	6	3		10	45	Morn.	
25	Wed	Annunciation B. V. M.	5	56	6	4		11	25	0	34
26	Thur	☾ highest.	5	55	6	5	♋	11	59	1	21
27	Frid	*Cloudy and*	5	54	6	6		morn		2	21
28	Satur	War with Russia, '54.	5	53	6	7	♌	0	40	3	29
29	*S.*	Palm Sun. *some rain.*	5	52	6	8		1	35	4	54
30	Mon	Regulus sou. 9h. 26m.	5	51	6	9	♍	2	20	6	11
31	Tues	Calhoun died, 1850.	5	50	6	10		3	45	7	16

[4th Month,]   APRIL, 1863.   [30 Days.

MOON'S PHASES.

	D.	H.	M.
Full Moon	3	11	3 eve.
Last Quarter	10	9	14 eve
New Moon	17	9	47 eve.
First Quarter	25	8	22 eve.

6 A miller has a head of water four feet above the sluice, how high must the water be raised above the opening so that half as much again water may be discharged from the sluice in the same time?

D. of M	D. of W	Various Phenomena.	Sun rises H.M.	Sun sets H.M.	MOON'S PLACE.	Moon ri&sts H. M.	High tide Savannah H. M.
1	Wed	Regulus sou. 9h. 18m.	5 49	6 11	♎	4 35	8 4
2	Thur	Pleasant weather.	5 48	6 12		5 2	8 42
3	Frid	Good Friday for	5 47	6 13	♏	rises.	9 16
4	Satur	W. H. Harrison d'd '41.	5 46	6 14		7 0	9 48
5	S	East. Sunday [planting.	5 45	6 15	♐	7 58	10 19
6	Mon	Easter Monday.	5 44	6 16		8 36	10 48
7	Tues	☾ lowest.	5 43	6 17	♑	9 21	11 20
8	Wed	Rain with Thunder.	5 42	6 18		10 20	11 42
9	Thur	Edward IV. died 1483.	5 41	6 19		11 18	E. 27
10	Frid	Bat. of Toulouse, 1814.	5 40	6 20	♒	morn.	1 8
11	Satur	Pittsburg burned, 1845.	5 39	6 21		0 15	1 57
12	S.	♄ ☍ ☉ ♃ rises 6h. 22m.	5 38	6 22	♓	1 21	2 58
13	Mon	Fort Sumter taken, '61.	5 37	6 23		2 26	4 18
14	Tues	Embargo repealed 1814	5 36	6 24		3 35	5 33
15	Wed	Spica sou. 11h. 39m.	5 35	6 25	♈	4 50	6 43
16	Thur	Warm for this	5 34	6 26		5 52	7 37
17	Frid	Virginia seceded, 1861.	5 33	6 27	♉	sets.	8 29
18	Satur	month.	5 32	6 28		7 30	9 11
19	S.	☉ enters ♉. [near.	5 31	6 29	♊	8 18	9 59
20	Mon	☾ ☌ ♀ at 2h 8m aft. very	5 30	6 30		9 0	10 47
21	Tues	Cloudy and	5 29	6 31		9 42	11 32
22	Wed	☾ highest. windy,	5 28	6 32	♋	10 31	Morn.
23	Thur	St. George.	5 27	6 33		11 14	0 17
24	Frid	Brazil discovered, 1500.	5 26	6 34	♌	11 58	1 5
25	Satu	St. Mark. Fair and	5 25	6 35		morn.	2 1
26	S.	Spica sou. 10h. 56m.	5 24	6 36	♍	0 40	3 2
27	Mon	Arcturus sou. 11h. 44m.	5 23	6 37		1 31	4 18
28	Tues	Wolfe killed, 1759.	5 22	6 38	♎	2 22	5 26
29	Wed	pleasant weather.	5 21	6 39		3 11	6 32
30	Thur	Washington inaug. '89.	5 20	6 40	♏	4 0	7 25

[5th Month,] MAY, 1863. [31 Days.

MOON'S PHASES.

	D.	H.	M.
Full Moon	3	9	43 mo.
Last Quarter	10	5	10 mo.
New Moon	17	11	15 mo.
First Quarter	25	11	23 mo.

7. What is the velocity of water issuing from a head of water 5 feet deep?

8. What is the difference between the length of a pendulum, which vibrates half seconds, and one which swings 3 seconds?

D. of M	D of W	Various Phenomena.	Sun rises H.M.	Sun sets H.M.	MOON'S PLACE	Moon ri.&sts H. M.	High tide Savannah H. M.
1	Frid	St. Philip & St. James.	5 20	6 40		4 52	8 6
2	Satur	*Warm and dry*	5 19	6 41	♐	5 46	8 46
3	S.	Tennessee seceded '61.	5 18	6 42		rises.	9 20
4	Mon	Robert Grier died, '48.	5 17	6 43		8 0	9 53
5	Tues	Moon lowest. *Damp*	5 16	6 44	♑	8 50	10 25
6	Wed	Humboldt died '59.	5 15	6 45		9 41	10 59
7	Thur	*and much*	5 15	6 45	♒	10 36	11 33
8	Frid	*cloudy weather.*	5 14	6 46		11 21	E. 9
9	Satur	Arcturus sou 10h 56m.	5 13	6 47	♓	11 59	0 52
10	S.	Rogation Sunday.	5 12	6 48		morn.	1 42
11	Mon	*Rain with*	5 12	6 48		0 46	2 38
12	Tues	Antares sou 1h 0m.	5 11	6 49	♈	1 32	3 46
13	Wed	*thunder.*	5 10	6 50		2 25	4 59
14	Thur	Ascension day.	5 9	6 51	♉	3 36	6 4
15	Frid	*Now we may*	5 9	6 51		4 41	7 6
16	Satur	*expect*	5 8	6 52		5 58	8 1
17	S.	Sun eclipsed invisible.	5 7	6 53	♊	sets.	8 51
18	Mon	*a fine growing*	5 7	6 53		8 2	9 44
19	Tues	Moon highest.	5 6	6 54	♋	8 51	10 32
20	Wed	Sun enters ♊ *season.*	5 6	6 55		9 40	11 16
21	Thur	*till the end*	5 5	6 55	♌	10 36	Morn.
22	Frid	*of this*	5 4	6 56		10 50	0 16
23	Satur	Irish rebellion com. '98.	5 4	6 56	♍	11 31	0 59
24	S.	Whit Sunday.	5 3	6 57		11 58	1 38
25	Mon	Whit Monday. *month.*	5 3	6 57	♎	morn.	2 30
26	Tues	John Calvin died, 1564.	5 2	6 58		0 52	3 28
27	Wed	*Fair*	5 2	6 58		1 47	4 35
28	Thur	*and pleasant.*	5 1	6 59	♏	2 35	5 37
29	Frid	Gen. Putnam died, '90.	5 1	6 59		3 21	6 36
30	Satur	Alex. Pope died, 1744.	5 0	7 0	♐	4 15	7 31
31	S.	Trinity Sunday.	5 0	7 0		5 20	8 14

6th Month.]   JUNE, 1863.   [30 Days.

MOON'S PHASES.

	D.	H.	M.
Full Moon	1	6	1 eve.
Last Quarter	8	1	13 eve.
New Moon	16	1	54 mo.
First Quarter	24	0	19 mo.

9. I observed, that while a stone was falling from a precipice, a string, with a bullet at the end, which measured 25 inches to the middle of the ball, had made five vibrations, what was the height of the precipice?

D. of M	D of W	Various Phenomena.	Sun rises H.M.	Sun sets H.M.	MOON'S PLACE.	Moon ri & sts H. M.	High tide Savannah H. M.
1	Mon	Moon eclipsed visible.	4 59	7 1	♑	ises.	8 54
2	Tues	Moon lowest. *Pleasant*	4 59	7 1		8 0	9 29
3	Wed	Transit of ♀ in 1769.	4 58	7 2	♒	8 50	10 7
4	Thur	*weather.*	4 58	7 2		9 42	10 43
5	Frid	Dr. Worcester died '21.	4 58	7 2		10 31	11 17
6	Satur	*Cloudy and some*	4 57	7 3	♓	11 22	11 56
7	S.	Antares sou 11h 13m.	4 57	7 3		11 50	E. 39
8	Mon	Gen. Jackson died '45.	4 57	7 3	♈	Morn.	1 26
9	Tues	S. L. Southard born '87.	4 57	7 3		0 43	2 19
10	Wed	Victory at Bethel, 1861.	4 56	7 4	♉	1 37	3 20
11	Thur	St. Barnabas. *rain.*	4 56	7 4		2 25	4 30
12	Frid	*Warm*	4 56	7 4	♊	3 25	5 35
13	Satur	*and unpleasant.*	4 56	7 4		4 35	6 43
14	S.	Moon highest.	4 56	7 4		5 40	7 45
15	Mon	*Rain with thunder.*	4 56	7 4	♋	6 48	8 40
16	Tues	Pres. Polk died, 1849.	4 55	7 5		sets.	9 32
17	Wed	Bat. Bunker Hill, 1775.	4 55	7 5	♌	8 25	10 20
18	Thur	Bat. Waterloo, 1815.	4 55	7 5		9 1	11 4
19	Frid	*More pleasant*	4 55	7 5	♍	9 50	11 46
20	Satur	Q. Vict. crowned, '37.	4 55	7 5		10 20	Morn.
21	S.	Sun ent. ♋. Longest day.	4 55	7 5		10 41	0 28
22	Mon	Antares sou 10h 14m.	4 55	7 5	♎	11 10	1 6
23	Tues	Akenside died, 1772.	4 55	7 5		11 56	1 54
24	Wed	St. John Baptist.	4 55	7 5	♏	Morn.	2 40
25	Thur	Bish. Gadsden died, '52.	4 55	7 5		0 43	3 3
26	Frid	Bat. Fort Moul. 1776.	4 55	7 5	♐	1 31	4 39
27	Satur	Monmouth Bat. 1778.	4 56	7 4		2 33	5 42
28	S.	*Warm and*	4 56	7 4		3 41	6 44
29	Mon	☾ lowest. St. Peter.	4 56	7 4	♑	4 58	7 40
30	Tues	*dry weather.*	4 56	7 4		6 0	8 25

7th Month.]   **JULY, 1863.**   **[31 Days**

MOON'S PHASES.

	D.	H.	M.
Full Moon	1	1	6 mo.
Last Quarter	7	10	17 eve.
New Moon	15	5	3 eve.
First Quarter	23	10	58 mo.
Full Moon	30	7	38 mo.

10. There is a sluice, one end of which is 2 1-2 feet lower than the other, what is the velocity of the stream per second?

11. If a ball fall through a space of 484 feet in 5 1-2 seconds, with what velocity will it strike?

D. of M	D of W	Various Phenomena.	Sun rises H.M.	Sun sets H.M.	MOON'S PLACE	Moon ri.&sts H. M.	High tide Savannah H. M.
1	Wed	Sultry weather.	4 56	7 4		rises.	9 7
2	Thur	Vis. of B. V. Mary.	4 56	7 4	♒	8 31	9 46
3	Frid	Fort Erie taken, 1814.	4 57	7 3		9 21	10 26
4	Satur	U. S. Dec. Indepen.'76.	4 57	7 3	♓	10 2	11 3
5	S.	Bat. Cheat Mount, '61.	4 58	7 2		10 54	11 42
6	Mon	Rain with loud	4 58	7 2		11 46	E. 24
7	Tues	thunder and	4 58	7 2	♈	morn.	1 8
8	Wed	Antares sou 9h 12m.	4 58	7 2		0 32	1 57
9	Thur	Pres. Taylor died 1850.	4 59	7 1	♉	1 25	2 54
10	Frid	Columbus born, 1447.	4 59	7 1		2 17	4 0
11	Satur	J. Q. Adams born, 1767.	4 59	7 1		3 21	5 15
12	S.	Hull invad. Canada,'12.	5 0	7 0	♊	4 0	6 30
13	Mon	vivid lightning.	5 0	7 0		4 38	7 37
14	Tues	Moon highest.	5 1	6 59	♋	5 0	8 33
15	Wed	Antares sou 8h 44m.	5 1	6 59		sets.	9 23
16	Thur	Hegira begins 622.	5 2	6 58	♌	7 38	10 8
17	Frid	Elbridge Gerry b. 1739.	5 2	6 58		8 26	10 48
18	Satur	Bat. Bull Run, 1861.	5 3	6 57	♍	9 15	11 24
19	S	Congress met at Rich'd	5 3	6 57		10 0	11 59
20	Mon	Vega sou 10h 36m. ['61	5 4	6 56	♎	10 48	Morn.
21	Tues	Bat. Manassas 1861.	5 5	6 55		11 21	0 36
22	Wed	Sun enters ♌.	5 6	6 55	♏	11 59	1 13
23	Thur	Warm	5 6	6 54		morn.	1 53
24	Frid	and	5 6	6 54	♐	0 48	2 34
25	Satur	St. James. dry	5 7	6 53		1 38	3 35
26	S.	St. Anne weather.	5 8	6 52		2 40	4 49
27	Mon	Moon lowest.	5 8	6 52	♑	3 44	6 2
28	Tues	Dog days begin.	5 9	6 51		4 56	7 8
29	Wed	Rainy and	5 10	6 50	♒	6 0	8 1
30	Thur	stormy.	5 11	6 49		rises.	8 45
31	Frid	Fomalhaut sou 2h 13m.	5 11	6 49	♓	8 21	9 26

8th Month,] AUGUST 1863. [31 Days.

MOON'S PHASES.

	D.	H.	M
Last Quarter	6	9	28 mo.
New Moon	14	8	27 mo.
First Quarter	21	8	12 eve.
Full Moon	28	3	19 eve.

12. If a ball strike the ground with a velocity of 56 feet per second, from what height did it fall?

13. In what time will a musket ball, dropped from the top of a steeple 484 feet high, come to the ground?

D. of M	D of W	Various Phenomena.	Sun rises H. M.	Sun sets H. M.	SNOOK PLACE	Moon ri & sts H. M.	Hi'h Tide Savannah H. M.
1	Satur	Lammac Day.	5 12	6 48		9 10	10 5
2	S.	Sweltry weather.	5 13	6 47		9 57	10 42
3	Mon	Burr's trial com. 1807.	5 13	6 47	♈	10 47	11 23
4	Tues	Brownstown Bat. 1812.	5 14	6 46		11 21	Even.5
5	Wed	Fomalhaut sou 1h 53m.	5 15	6 45	♉	11 54	0 47
6	Thur	Bat. Hang. Rock, 1780	5 16	6 44		Morn.	1 36
7	Frid	Rain and thunder.	5 17	6 43		0 41	2 2-
8	Satur	Cloudy and	5 17	6 43	♊	1 36	3 36
9	S.	Bat. Oak Hill, 1861.	5 18	6 42		2 25	4 58
10	Mon	Moon highest. windy	5 19	6 41	♋	3 35	6 20
11	Tues	weather,	5 20	6 40		4 45	7 30
12	Wed	George IV. born, 1762.	5 21	6 39	♌	5 55	8 23
13	Thur	Now we may	5 22	6 38		6 10	9 10
14	Frid	Altair sou 10h 9m.	5 22	6 38	♍	Sets.	9 50
15	Satur	Bonaparte born, 1769.	5 23	6 37		8 1	10 25
16	S.	Bat. at Camden, 1780.	5 24	6 36	♎	8 50	10 59
17	Mon	expect a heavy	5 25	6 35		9 31	11 32
18	Tues	Altair sou 9h 53m.	5 26	6 34	♏	10 22	Morn.
19	Wed	storm of wind and	5 27	6 33		11 10	0 16
20	Thur	Bat. in Mexico, 1847.	5 28	6 32	♐	11 50	0 36
21	Frid	Wm. IV. born, 1765.	5 29	6 31		Morn.	1 12
22	Satur	☉ enters ♍. rain.	5 30	6 30		0 40	1 51
23	S.	☾ lowest. [from N. E.	5 31	6 29	♑	1 31	2 44
24	Mon	♀ brightest in the eve.	5 32	6 28		2 21	3 57
25	Tues	Bp. Bowen died 1839.	5 33	6 27	♒	3 25	5 17
26	Wed	Dr. Adam Clark d. '32.	5 34	6 26		4 15	6 32
27	Thur	Fair and mild.	5 35	6 25		5 16	7 31
28	Frid	Hatteras taken 1861.	5 36	6 24	♓	Rises.	8 18
29	Satur	St. John Bap. beheaded	5 37	6 23		7 31	9 2
30	S.	Paley born, 1743.	5 38	6 22	♈	8 15	9 41
31	Mon	Bunyan died, 1688.	5 39	5 21		9 0	10 20

9th Month,] **SEPTEMBER, 1863.** **[30 Days.**

MOON'S PHASES.

	D.	H.	M.
Last Quarter	4	11	13 eve.
New Moon	12	11	29 eve.
First Quarter	20	4	41 mo.
Full Moon	27	0	32 mo.

14. If the attraction of the moon raise a tide on the earth five feet high, what will be the height of a tide, raised by the earth on the surface of the moon, under similar circumstances.

D. of M	D. of W	Various Phenomena.	Sun rises H.M.	Sun sets H.M.	MOON'S PLACE	Moon ri &sts H. M.	H. Tide SAVANNAH H. M.
1	Tues	Fair and warm.	5 39	6 21		9 40	11 0
2	Wed	London burn'd, 1666.	5 40	6 20	♉	10 20	11 44
3	Thur	Cloudy, and some	5 41	6 19		11 10	ev. 27
4	Frid	Altair S. 8 h'rs 46 min.	5 42	6 18	♊	morn.	1 15
5	Satur	Dog-days end. rain	5 43	6 17		0 2	2 9
6	S.	Lafayette, born, 1757.	5 44	6 16		0 58	3 20
7	Mon	☽ highest. with thun-	5 45	6 15	♋	1 43	4 46
8	Tues	Bat. Eutaw, 1781. der.	5 46	6 14		2 56	6 10
9	Wed	Fomalhaut sou. 11h 32m	5 47	6 13	♌	3 2	7 18
10	Thur	Bat. Lake Erie, 1813.	5 48	6 12		4 15	8 8
11	Frid	Cloudy and	5 49	6 11	♍	5 25	8 49
12	Satur	damp.	5 50	6 10		sets.	9 25
13	S.	Donati's Comet, 1858.	5 51	6 9	♎	7 0	9 59
14	Mon	Moscow burned, 1812.	5 52	6 8		7 54	10 30
15	Tues	Surren. of N. Y., 1776.	5 53	6 7	♏	8 43	11 1
16	Wed	Fomalhaut sou. 11h 4m.	5 54	6 6		9 31	11 32
17	Thur	Changeable and	5 55	6 5	♐	10 20	morn.
18	Frid	unsettled weather.	5 56	6 4		11 5	0 16
19	Satur	Moon lowest.	5 57	6 3	♑	11 56	0 36
20	S.	Stormy and boisterous.	5 58	6 2		morn.	1 16
21	Mon	St. Matthew.	5 59	6 1	♒	0 43	2 5
22	Tues	Weather may now	6 0	6 0		1 32	3 10
23	Wed	Sun enters ♎. Days and	6 1	5 59		2 37	4 36
24	Thur	[nights equal.	6 2	5 58	♓	3 46	5 54
25	Frid	Fomalhaut sou. 10h 29m	6 3	5 57		4 28	7 1
26	Satur	be expected fair.	6 4	5 56	♈	5 29	7 49
27	S.	Artic lost, 1854.	6 5	5 55		rises.	8 33
28	Mon	Detroit retaken, 1813.	6 6	5 54		7 21	9 12
29	Tues	♀ ☌ Sun Inferior.	6 7	5 53	♉	8 10	9 55
30	Wed	♄ ☌ Sun. St. Jerome.	6 8	5 52		9 0	10 40

10th Month.]　　　OCTOBER, 1863.　　　[31 Days

MOON'S PHASES.

	D.	H.	M.	
Last Quarter	4	3	27	eve.
New Moon	12	1	27	eve.
First Quarter	19	1	34	eve.
Full Moon	26	0	31	eve.

15. Suppose a vessel 3 feet wide, 5 feet long and 4 feet high, what is the perpendicular pressure on the bottom, it being filled with water to the brim?

D. of M.	D. of W.	Various Phenomena.	Sun rises H. M.	Sun sets. H. M.	MOON'S PLACE	Moon ri & sts H. M.	High tide Savannah H. M.
1	Thur	♃ ☌ ♀　　Cloudy and	6 9	5 51	♊	9 56	11 24
2	Frid	Major Andre exe. 1780.	6 10	5 50		10 43	E. 11
3	Satur	damp weather.	6 11	5 49		11 36	0 58
4	S.	☾ highest.	6 12	5 48	♋	morn.	1 55
5	Mon	Brainard died, 1747.	6 13	5 47		0 21	3 4
6	Tues	Fomalhaut sou 9h 46m.	6 14	5 46	♌	1 15	4 27
7	Wed	Bat King's Mount. '80.	6 15	5 45		2 14	5 49
8	Thur	Cool nights and	6 15	5 45	♍	3 12	6 55
9	Frid	Battle Schleitz, 1806.	6 16	5 44		4 8	7 44
10	Satur	mornings.	6 17	5 43	♎	4 59	8 25
11	S.	Bahamas discov'd 1492.	6 18	5 42		5 48	8 59
12	Mon	Fair and	6 19	5 41	♏	sets.	9 32
13	Tues	mild weather.	6 20	5 40		6 21	10 3
14	Wed	Fomalhaut sou 9h 14m.	6 21	5 39	♐	7 22	10 34
15	Thur	Bank Panic, 1857.	6 22	5 38		8 28	11 6
16	Frid	Raining and	6 23	5 37	♑	9 36	11 37
17	Satur	Burgoyne surrend 1777.	6 24	5 36		10 42	Morn.
18	S.	St. Luke.　　stormy.	6 25	5 35		11 50	0 16
19	Mon	Cornwallis sur 1781.	6 26	5 34	♒	morn.	0 50
20	Tues	Windy and cool.	6 27	5 33		0 42	1 35
21	Wed	Fomalhaut sou 8h 47m.	6 28	5 32	♓	1 36	2 34
22	Thur	Now we may expect	6 29	5 31		2 39	3 53
23	Frid	☉ enters ♏.	6 30	5 30		3 21	5 9
24	Satur	frost.	6 31	5 29	♈	4 28	6 21
25	S.	7 ✷ sou 1h 23m.	6 32	5 28		5 41	7 16
26	Mon	Changeable and	6 33	5 27	♉	rises.	8 4
27	Tues	Fomalhaut sou 8h 23m.	6 34	5 26		7 1	8 49
28	Wed	St. Sim. and St. Jude.	6 35	5 25		7 58	9 35
29	Thur	unsettled.	6 36	5 24	♊	8 42	10 21
30	Frid	☾ highest.	6 37	5 23		9 31	11 7
31	Satur	♃ ☌ ☉　　weather.	6 38	5 22	♋	10 14	11 54

[11th Month.] NOVEMBER, 1863. [30 Days.

MOON'S PHASES.

	D.	H.	M.
Last Quarter	3	9	28 mo.
New Moon	11	2	36 mo.
First Quarter	17	11	29 eve.
Full Moon	25	3	29 mo.

16. With what velocity will an iron ball begin to descend, if raised 3,000 miles above the earth's surface?

17. How high must a ball be raised, to lose half its weight?

D. of M	D of W	Various Phenomena.	Sun rises H.M.	Sun sets H.M.	MOON'S PLACE	Moon ri & sts H. M.	H. Tide SAVANNAH. H. M.
1	S.	All Saint's day.	6 39	5 21		11 5	eve. 45
2	Mon	All Souls' day.	6 40	5 20		11 57	1 38
3	Tues	Fair and Cool.	6 40	5 20		morn.	2 38
4	Wed	♀ brightest in the morn.	6 41	5 19		0 43	3 53
5	Thur	Gunpowder plot, 1605.	6 42	5 18	♍	1 37	5 6
6	Frid	Leonard. Cloudy	6 43	5 17		2 36	6 15
7	Satur	Bat. Belmont, 1861.	6 44	5 16	♎	3 34	7 11
8	S.	Transit of ☿, 1848.	6 45	5 15		4 31	7 54
9	Mon	and Damp.	6 46	5 14	♏	5 21	8 33
10	Tues	Milton died, 1674.	6 46	5 14		6 2	9 8
11	Wed	● Eclipsed, invisible.	6 47	5 13	♐	sets.	9 42
12	Thur	Frosty and	6 48	5 12		6 31	10 13
13	Frid	Moon lowest. Fair.	6 49	5 11	♑	7 39	10 45
14	Satur	Chas. Carroll d., 1832.	6 49	5 11		8 36	11 18
15	S.	Witherspoon d., 1794.	6 50	5 10	♒	9 51	11 52
16	Mon	Tea dest'd Boston, 1773	6 51	5 9		10 59	morn.
17	Tues	7 Stars sou. 11h 49m.	6 52	5 8		morn.	0 31
18	Wed	Windy, and a Cold	6 52	5 8	♓	0 8	1 15
19	Thur	7 Stars sou. 11h 41m.	6 53	5 7		1 10	2 7
20	Frid	Rain may be expected.	6 54	5 6	♈	2 21	3 9
21	Satur	Sun enters ♐	6 54	5 6		3 36	4 25
22	S.	Fair, and	6 55	5 5		4 48	5 35
23	Mon	Bomb. Ft. Pickens, '61.	6 56	5 4	♉	5 35	6 42
24	Tues	Cold Winds.	6 56	5 4		6 25	7 38
25	Wed	Moon Eclipsed, visible.	6 57	5 3	♊	rises.	8 27
26	Thur	Q. Isabella died, 1504.	6 58	5 2		6 10	9 19
27	Frid	Moon highest.	6 58	5 2	♋	7 0	10 9
28	Satur	Cloudy Weather.	6 59	5 1		7 56	10 57
29	S	Advent Sunday.	6 59	5 1		8 43	11 42
30	Mon	St. Andrew's Day.	7 0	5 0	♌	9 30	eve. 29

12th Month.] **DECEMBER, 1863.** **[31 Days.**

MOON'S PHASES.

	D.	H.	M.
Last Quarter	3	3	53 mo.
New Moon	10	2	43 eve.
First Quarter	17	10	39 mo.
Full Moon	24	9	0 eve.

18. If the velocity of a stream of water spouting through the bulk head of a mill be 16 feet per second, what head of water is there?

D. of M	D. of W	Various Phenomena.	Sun rises H.M.	Sun sets H.M.	MOON'S PLACE	Moon ri.&sts H. M.	H. Tide SAVANNAH. H. M.
1	Tues	Days 10 hours long.	7 0	5 0		10 25	1 18
2	Wed	7 Stars souths 10h 50m.	7 1	4 59	♍	11 21	2 8
3	Thur	*Fair and Frosty.*	7 1	4 59		morn.	3 4
4	Frid	Sun fast. clock 9m 19s.	7 2	4 58	♎	0 15	4 12
5	Satur	*Rainy and Cool.*	7 2	4 58		1 25	5 18
6	S.	Van Buren born, 1782.	7 2	4 58	♏	2 35	6 24
7	Mon	*Windy and*	7 3	4 57		3 48	7 20
8	Tues	7 Stars souths 10h 26m.	7 3	4 57	♐	4 59	8 3
9	Wed	*unpleasant Weather.*	7 3	4 57		5 58	8 43
10	Thur	Moon lowest.	7 3	4 57	♑	sets.	9 21
11	Frid	Gt. Fire Charleston, '61.	7 4	4 56		5 56	9 56
12	Satur	*Cold enough*	7 4	4 56	♒	6 40	10 31
13	S.	Bat. Valley Mount.,1861	7 4	4 56		7 28	11 5
14	Mon	Washington died, 1799.	7 4	4 56		8 45	11 40
15	Tues	*for Ice.*	7 4	4 56	♓	9 40	morn.
16	Wed	Gt. Fire N. York, 1835.	7 5	4 55		10 53	0 17
17	Thur	*Rainy and unpleasant*	7 5	4 55	♈	morn.	1 0
18	Frid	Sun fast. clock 2m 51s.	7 5	4 55		0 2	1 50
19	Satur	*Weather.*	7 5	4 55		1 12	2 59
20	S.	S. Carolina seced. '60.	7 5	4 55	♉	2 21	4 25
21	Mon	Sun ent. ♑ Shortest day.	7 5	4 55		3 42	5 35
22	Tues	Land. of Pilgrims, 1620.	7 5	4 55	♊	4 56	6 42
23	Wed	Sir I. Newton born,1642	7 5	4 55		6 2	7 38
24	Thur	Sun & clock agree.	7 5	4 55		rises.	8 27
25	Frid	CHRISTMAS DAY. *Clear*	7 5	4 55	♋	5 58	9 10
26	Satur	☽ highest. St. Stephen.	7 5	4 55		6 48	10 9
27	S.	St. John Evang. *and*	7 4	4 56	♌	7 37	10 57
28	Mon	Innocents. *cold weather*	7 4	4 56		8 26	11 42
29	Tues	The Java taken, 1812.	7 4	4 56	♍	9 13	eve.26
30	Wed	7 Stars souths 9h 0m.	7 4	4 56		10 14	1 19
31	Thur	*for this Climate.*	7 4	4 56	♎	11 12	2 10

CONSTITUTION

OF THE

CONFEDERATE STATES OF AMERICA.

We, the people of the Confederate States, each State acting in its sovereign and independent character, in order to form a permanent federal government, establish justice, insure domestic tranquility, and secure the blessings of liberty to ourselves and our posterity—invoking the favor and guidance of Almighty God—do ordain and establish this Constitution for the Confederate States of America.

ARTICLE I.

SECTION I.

All legislative powers herein delegated shall be vested in a Congress of the Confederate States, which shall consist of a Senate and House of Representatives.

SECTION II.

1. The House of Representatives shall be composed of members chosen every second year, by the people of the several States; and the elections in each State shall be citizens of the Confederate States, and have the qualifications requisite for electors of the most numerous branch of the State Legislature; but no person of foreign birth, not a citizen of the Confederate States, shall be allowed to vote for any officer, civil or political, State or Federal.

2. No person shall be a Representative who shall not have attained the age of twenty-five years, and be a citizen of the Confederate States, and who shall not, when elected, be an inhabitant of that State in which he shall be chosen.

3. Representatives and Direct Taxes shall be apportioned among the several States, which may be included within this Confederacy, according to their respective numbers, which shall be determined by adding to the whole number of free persons, including those bound to service for a term of years, and including Indians not taxed three-fifths of all slaves. The actual enumeration shall be made within three years after the first meeting of the Congress of Confederate States, and within every subsequent term of ten years, in such manner as they shall, by law, direct. The number of Representatives shall not exceed one for every fifty thousand, but each State shall have at least one Representative; and until such enumeration shall be made, the State of South Carolina shall be

entitled to choose six—the State of Georgia, ten—the State of Alabama, nine—the State of Florida, two—the State of Mississippi, seven—the State of Louisiana, six—and the State of Texas, six.

4. When vacancies happen in the representation from any State the Executive authority thereof shall issue writs of election to fill such vacancies.

5. The House of Representatives shall choose their Speaker and other officers; and shall have the sole power of impeachment: except that any judicial or other federal officers resident and acting solely within the limits of any State, may be impeached by a vote of two-thirds of both branches of the Legislature thereof.

SECTION III.

1. The Senate of the Confederate States shall be composed of two Senators from each State, chosen for six years by the Legislature thereof, at the regular session next immediately preceding the commencement of the term of service; and each Senator shall have one vote.

2. Immediately after they shall be assembled, in consequence of the first election, they shall be divided as equally as possible into three classes. The seats of the Senators of the first class shall be vacated at the expiration of the second year; of the second class at the expiration of the fourth year; and of the third class, at the expiration of the sixth year; so that one-third may be chosen every second year; and if vacancies happen by resignation, or otherwise, during the recess of the Legislature of any State, the Executive thereof may make temporary appointments until the next meeting of the Legislature, which shall then fill such vacancies.

3. No person shall be a Senator who shall not have attained the age of thirty years, and be a citizen of the Confederate States; and who shall not when elected, be an inhabitant of the State for which he shall be chosen.

4. The Vice President of the Confederate States shall be President of the Senate, but shall have no vote, unless they shall be equally divided.

5. The Senate shall choose their other officers; and also a President *pro tempore* in the absence of the Vice President, or when he shall exercise the office of President of the Confederate States.

6. The Senate shall have the sole power to try all impeachments. When sitting for that purpose, they shall be on oath or affirmation. When the President of the Confederate States is tried, the Chief Justice shall preside; and no person shall be convicted without the concurrence of two thirds of the members present.

7. Judgment in cases of impeachment shall not extend further than to removal from office, and disqualification to hold and enjoy any office of honor or profit, under the Confederate States; but the party convicted shall, nevertheless, be liable and subject to indictment, trial, judgment, and punishment according to law.

SECTION IV.

1. The time, place, and manner of holding elections for Senators and Representatives shall be prescribed in each State by the Legislature thereof, subject to the provisions of this Constitution: but the Congress may, at any time, by law, make or alter such regulations, except as to the times and places of choosing Senators.
2. The Congress shall assemble at least once in every year, and such meeting shall be on the first Monday in December, unless they shall, by law, appoint a different day.

SECTION V.

1. Each House shall be the judge of the elections, returns, and qualifications of its own members, and a majority of each shall constitute a quorum to do business; but a smaller number may adjourn from day to day, and may be authorized to compel the attendance of absent members, in such manner, and under such penalties as each House may provide.
2. Each House may determine the rule of its proceedings, punish its members for disorderly behavior, and with the concurrence of two-thirds of the whole number, expel a member.
3. Each House shall keep a Journal of its proceedings, and from time to time publish the same, excepting such parts as may, in their judgment, require secrecy; and the yeas and nays of the members of either House, on any question, shall, at the desire of one-fifth of those present, be entered on the journal.
4. Neither House, during the session of Congress, shall, without the consent of the other, adjourn for more than three days, nor to any other place than that in which the two Houses shall be sitting.

SECTION VI.

1. The Senators and Representatives shall receive a compensation for their services, to be ascertained by law, and paid out of the Treasury of the Confederate States. They shall, in all cases, except treason, and breach of the peace, be privileged from arrest during their attendance at the session of their respective Houses, and in going to and returning from the same; and for any speech, or debate in either House, they shall not be questioned in any other place.
2. No Senator or Representative shall, during the time for which he was elected, be appointed to any civil office under the authority of the Confederate States, which shall have been created, or the emoluments whereof shall have been increased during such time; and no person holding any office under the Confederate States shall be a member of either House during his continuance in office. But

Congress may, by law, grant to the principal officer in each of the Executive Departments a seat upon the floor of either House, with the privilege of discussing any measures appertaining to his department.

SECTION VII.

1. All bills for raising revenue shall originate in the House of Representatives; but the Senate may propose or concur with amendments, as on other bills.

2. Every bill which shall have passed both Houses, shall, before it becomes a law, be presented to the President of the Confederate States; if he approve, he shall sign it; but if not, he shall return it, with his objections, to the House in which it shall have originated, who shall enter the objections at large on their journals, and proceed to reconsider it. If, after such reconsideration, two-thirds of that House shall agree to pass the bill, it shall be sent, together with the objections, to the other House, by which it shall likewise be reconsidered; and if approved by two-thirds of that House, it shall become a law. But in all such cases, the votes of both Houses shall be determined by yeas and nays, and the persons voting for or against the bill shall be entered on the Journal of each House respectively. If any bill shall not be returned by the President within ten days (Sundays excepted) after it shall have been presented to him, the same shall be a law in like manner as if he had signed it, unless the Congress, shall by their adjournment, prevent its return; in which case it shall not be a law. The President may approve any appropriation, and disapprove any other appropriation in the same bill. In such case, he shall, in signing the bill, designate the appropriations disapproved; and shall return a copy of such appropriations, with his objections, to the House in which the bill shall have originated, and the same proceedings shall then be had as in case of other bills disapproved by the President.

3. Every order, resolution, or vote, to which the concurrence of both Houses may be necessary (except on a question of adjournment) shall be presented to the President of the Confederate States; and before the same shall take effect, shall be approved by him; or being disapproved by him may be repassed by two-thirds of both Houses, according to the rules and limitations prescribed in case of a bill.

SECTION VIII.

The Congress shall have power—

1. To lay and collect taxes, duties, imposts and excises, for revenue necessary to pay the debts, provide for the common defence, and carry on the Government of the Confederate States; but no bounties shall be granted from the treasury; nor shall any duties,

or taxes on importations from foreign nations be laid to promote or foster any branch of industry; and all duties, imposts and excises shall be uniform throughout the Confederate States:

2. To borrow money on the credit of the Confederate States:

3. To regulate commerce with foreign nations, and among the several States, and with the Indian tribes; but neither this, nor any other clause contained in the Constitution shall ever be construed to delegate the power to Congress to appropriate money for any internal improvement intended to facilitate commerce, except for the purpose of furnishing lights, beacons and buoys, and other aids to navigation upon the coast, and the improvement of harbors; and the removing of obstructions in river navigation, in all which cases, such duties shall be laid on the navigation facilitated thereby, as may be necessary to pay the costs and expenses thereof:

4. To establish uniform laws of naturalization, and uniform laws on the subject of bankruptcies, throughout the Confederate States; but no law of Congress shall discharge any debt contracted before the passage of the same:

5. To coin money, regulate the value thereof, and of foreign coin, and fix the standard of weights and measures:

6. To provide for the punishment of counterfeiting the securities and current coin of the Confederate States:

7. To establish post offices and post routes; but the expenses of the Postoffice Department, after the first day of March, in the year of our Lord, eighteen hundred and sixty-three, shall be paid out of its own revenues:

8. To promote the progress of science and useful arts, by securing for limited times to authors and inventors the exclusive right to their respective writings and discoveries:

9. To constitute tribunals inferior to the Supreme Court:

10. To define and punish piracies and felonies committed on the high seas, and offences against the law of nations:

11. To declare war, grant letters of marque and reprisal, and make rules concerning captures on land and water:

12. To raise and support armies; but no appropriation of money to that use shall be for a longer term than two years:

13. To provide and maintain a navy:

14. To make rules for government and the regulation of the land and naval forces:

15. To provide for calling forth the militia to execute the laws of the Confederate States, suppress insurrections and repel invasions:

16. To provide for organizing, arming and disciplining the militia, and for governing such part of them as may be employed in the service of the Confederate States; reserving to the States, respectively, the appointment of the officers, and the authority of

training the militia according to the discipline prescribed by Congress:

17. To exercise exclusive legislation, in all cases whatsoever, over such district (not exceeding ten miles square) as may, by cession of one or more States, and the acceptance of Congress, become the seat of the Government of the Confederate States; and to exercise like authority over all the places purchased by the consent of the legislature of the State in which the same shall be, for the erection of forts, magazines, arsenals, dockyards, and other needful buildings; and

18. To make all laws which shall be necessary and proper for carrying into execution the foregoing powers, and all other powers vested by this Constitution in the Government of the Confederate States, or in any department or office thereof.

SECTION IX.

1. The importation of negroes of the African race, from any foreign country, other than the slaveholding States or Territories of the United States of America, is hereby forbidden; and Congress is required to pass such laws as shall effectually prevent the same:

2. Congress shall also have power to prohibit the introduction of slaves from any State not a member of, or Territory not belonging to, this Confederacy.

3. The privilege of the writ of habeas corpus shall not be suspended, unless when, in cases of rebellion, or invasion, the public safety may require it.

4. No bill of attainder, or *ex post facto* law, or law denying or impairing the right of property in negro slaves, shall be passed.

5. No capitation or other direct tax shall be laid, unless in proportion to the census or enumeration hereinbefore directed to be taken.

6. No tax or duty shall be laid on articles exported from any State, except by a vote of two-thirds of both Houses.

7. No preference shall be given by any regulation of commerce or revenue to the ports of one State over those of another.

8. No money shall be drawn from the Treasury, but in consequence of appropriations made by law, and a regular statement and account of the receipts and expenditures of all public money shall be published from time to time.

9. Congress shall appropriate no money from the Treasury, except by a vote of two-thirds of both houses, taken by yeas and nays, unless it be asked and estimated for by some one of the heads of the Department, and submitted to Congress by the President; or for the purpose of paying its own expenses and contingencies; or for the payment of claims against the Confederate States, the justice of which shall have been judicially declared by a tribunal for

the investigation of claims against the Government, which it is hereby made the duty of Congress to establish.

10. All bills appropriating money shall specify in **Federal currency** the exact amount of each appropriation, and the purposes for which it is made; and Congress shall grant no extra compensation to any public contractor, officer, agent or servant, after such contract shall have been made, or such service rendered.

11. No title of nobility shall be granted by the Confederate States; and no person holding any office of profit or trust under them, shall, without the consent of the Congress, accept of any present, emoluments, office, or titles of any kind whatever, from any king, prince, or foreign State.

12. Congress shall make no law respecting an establishment of religion, or prohibiting the free exercise thereof; or abridging the freedom of speech or of the press; or the right of the people peaceably to assemble and petition the Government for a redress of grievances.

13. A well regulated militia being necessary to the security of a free State, the right of the people to keep and bear arms shall not be infringed.

14. No soldier shall, in time of peace, be quartered in any house without the consent of the owner; nor in time of war, but in a manner to be prescribed by law.

15. The right of the people to be secure in their persons, houses, papers, and effects, against unreasonable searches and seizures, shall not be violated; and no warrant shall issue but upon probable cause, supported by oath or affirmation, and particularly describing the place to be searched, and the person or things to be seized.

16. No person shall be held to answer for a capital or otherwise infamous crime, unless on a presentment or indictment of a grand jury, except in cases arising in the land or naval forces, or in the militia, when in actual service, in time of war or public danger; nor shall any person be subject for the same offence to be twice put in jeopardy of life or limb; nor be compelled, in any criminal case, to be a witness against himself; nor be deprived of life, liberty or property, without due process of law; nor shall private property be taken for public use, without just compensation.

17. In all criminal prosecutions the accused shall enjoy the right to a speedy and public trial, by an impartial jury of the State and district wherein the crime shall have been committed, which district shall have been previously ascertained by law, and to be informed of the nature and cause of the accusation; to be confronted with the witnesses against him; to have compulsory process for obtaining witnesses in his favor; and to have the assistance of counsel for his defence.

18. In suits at common law where the value in controversy shall exceed twenty dollars, the right of trial by jury shall be pre-

served; and no fact so tried by a jury shall be otherwise re-examined in any court of the Confederacy, than according to the rules of the common law.

19. Excessive bail shall not be required, nor excessive fines be imposed, nor cruel and unjust punishments be inflicted.

20. Every law, or resolution having the force of law, shall relate to but one subject, and that shall be expressed in the title.

SECTION X.

1. No State shall enter into any treaty, alliance, or confederation: grant letters of marque and reprisal; coin money, make anything but gold and silver coin a tender in payment of debts; pass any bill of attainder, or *ex post facto law*, or law impairing the obligation of contracts; or grant any title of nobility.

2. No state shall, without the consent of the Congress, lay any imposts, or duties on imposts or exports, except what may be absolutely necessary for executing its inspection laws; and the net produce of all duties and imposts, laid by any State on imports or exports, shall be for the use of the treasury of the Confederate States; and all such laws shall be subject to the revision and control of Congress.

3. No state shall, without the consent of Congress lay any duty of tonnage, except on sea-going vessels, for the improvement of its rivers and harbors navigated by the said vessels; but such duties shall not conflict with any treaties of the Confederate States with foreign nations; and any surplus or revenue thus derived, shall, after making such improvements, be paid into the common treasury; nor shall any State keep troops or ships of war in time of peace, enter into any agreement or compact with another State, or with a foreign power, or engage in war, unless actually invaded, or in such imminent danger as will not admit of delay. But when any river divides or flows through two or more States, they may enter into compacts with each other to improve the navigation thereof.

ARICLE II.

SECTION I.

1. The executive power shall be vested in a President of the Confederate States of America. He and the Vice-President shall hold their offices for the term of six years; but the President shall not be re-eligible. The President and Vice-President shall be elected as follows:

2. Each State shall appoint, in such manner as the Legislature thereof may direct, a number of electors equal to the whole number of Senators and Representatives to which the State may be entitled in the Congress; but no Senator or Representative, or

person holding an office of trust or profit under the Confederate States shall be appointed an elector.

3. The electors shall meet in their respective States and vote by ballot for President and Vice-President, one of whom, at least, shall not be an inhabitant of the same State with themselves; they shall name in their ballots the persons voted for as President, and in distinct ballots the person voted for as Vice-President, and they shall make distinct lists of all persons voted for as President, and of all persons voted for as Vice-President, and of the number of votes for each, which list they shall sign and certify, and transmit, sealed, to the government of the Confederate States, directed to the President of the Senate; the President of the Senate shall, in the presence of the Senate and House of Representatives, open all the certificates, and the vote shall then be counted; the person having the greatest number of votes for President shall be the President, if such number be a majority of the whole number of electors appointed: and if no person have such majority, then from the persons having the highest numbers, not exceeding three, on the list of those voted for as President, the House of Representatives shall choose immediately, by ballot, the President. But in choosing the President, the vote shall be taken by States, the representation from each State having one vote; a quorum for this purpose shall consist of a member or members from two-thirds of the States, and a majority of all the States shall be necessary to a choice. And if the House of Representatives shall not choose a President, whenever the right of choice shall devolve upon them, before the fourth day of March next following, then the Vice-President shall act as President, as in case of the death or other Constitutional disability of the President.

4. The person having the greatest number of votes as Vice-President shall be the Vice-President, if such number be a majority of the whole number of electors appointed, and if no person have a majority, then from the two highest numbers on the list of the Senate shall choose the Vice-President; a quorum for the purpose shall consist of two-thirds of the whole number of Senators, and a majority of the whole number shall be necessary to a choice.

5. No person constitutionally ineligible to the office of President shall be eligible to that of Vice-President of the Confederate States.

6. The Congress may determine the time of choosing the electors, and the day on which they shall give their votes; which day shall be the same throughout the Confederate States.

7. No person except a natural born citizen of the Confederate States, or a citizen thereof, at the time of the adoption of the Constitution, or a citizen thereof born in the United States prior to the 20th of December, 1860, shall be eligible to the office of President; neither shall any person be eligible to that office who shall

not have attained the age of thirty-five years, and been fourteen years a resident within the limits of the Confederate States, as they may exist at the time of his election.

8. In case of the removal of the President from office, or of his death, resignation, or inability to discharge the powers and duties of the said office, the same shall devolve on the Vice-President; and the Congress may, by law, provide for the case of removal, death, resignation or inability, both of the President and Vice-President, declaring what officer shall then act as President, and such officer shall act accordingly until the disability be removed or a President shall be elected.

9. The President shall, at stated times, receive for his services a compensation which shall neither be increased nor diminished during the period for which he shall have been elected: and he shall not receive within that period any other emolument from the Confederate States, or any of them.

10. Before he enters on the execution of his office, he shall take the following oath or affirmation:

"I do solemnly swear—or affirm—that I will faithfully execute the office of President of the Confederate States, and will, to the best of my ability, preserve, protect and defend the Constitution thereof."

SECTION II.

1. The President shall be Commander-in-Chief of the army and navy of the Confederate States, and of the militia of the several States, when called into the actual service of the Confederate States; he may require the opinion, in writing, of the principal officer in each of the Executive Departments, upon any subject relating to the duties of their respective offices; and he shall have power to grant reprieves and pardons for offences against the Confederate States, except in cases of impeachment.

2. He shall have power, by and with the advice and consent of the Senate, to make treaties, provided two-thirds of the Senators present concur, and he shall nominate, and by and with the advice and consent of the Senate, shall appoint ambassaders, other public ministers and consuls, Judges of the Supreme Court, and all other officers of the Confederate States, whose appointments are not herein otherwise provided for, and which shall be established by law; but the Congress may, by law, vest the appointment of such inferior officers, as they think proper, in the President alone, in the Courts of Law, or in the heads of Departments.

3. The principal in each of the Executive Departments, and all persons connected with the diplomatic service, may be removed from office at the pleasure of the President. All other civil officers of the Executive Department may be removed at any time by the President, or other appointing power, when their services are

unnecessary, or for dishonesty, incapacity, inefficiency, misconduct, or neglect of duty; and when so removed, the removal shall be reported to the Senate, together with the reasons therefor.

4. The President shall have power to fill all vacancies that may happen during the recess of the Senate, by granting commissions which shall expire at the end of their next session; but no person rejected by the Senate shall be re-appointed to the same office during their ensuing recess.

SECTION III.

1. The President shall, from time to time, give to the Congress information of the state of the Confederacy, and recommend to their consideration such measures as he shall judge necessary and expedient; he may, on extraordinary occasions, convene both Houses, or either of them; and in case of disagreement between them, with respect to the time of adjournment, he may adjourn them to such time as he shall think proper; he shall receive ambassadors and other public ministers; he shall take care that the laws be faithfully executed, and shall commission all the officers of the Confederate States.

SECTION IV.

1. The President, Vice-President, and all civil officers of the Confederate States, shall be removed from office on impeachment for, and conviction of treason, bribery, or other high crimes and misdemeanors.

ARTICLE III.

SECTION I.

1. The judicial power of the Confederate States shall be vested in one Superior Court, and in such Inferior Courts as the Congress may from time to time order and establish. The judges, both of the Superior and Inferior Courts, shall hold their offices during good behavior, and shall, at stated times, receive for the services a compensation, which shall not be diminished during their continuance in office.

SECTION II.

1. The judicial power shall extend to all cases arising under this Constitution, the laws of the Confederate States, and treaties made, or which shall be made, under their authority; to all cases affecting ambassadors, other public ministers and consuls; to all cases of admiralty and maritime jurisdiction; to controversies to which the Confederate States shall be a party: to controversies between two or more States; between a State and citizens of

another State, where the State is plaintiff; between citizens claiming lands under grants from different States; and between the State or the citizens thereof, and foreign States, citizens or subjects; but no State shall be sued by a citizen or subject of any foreign State.

2. In all cases affecting ambassadors, other public ministers, and consults, and those in which a State shall be a party, the Supreme Court shall have original jurisdiction. In all other cases beforementioned, the Supreme Court shall have appelate jurisdiction, both as to law and facts, with such exceptions, and under such regulations as the Congress shall make.

3. The trial of all crimes, except in cases of impeachment, shall be by jury, and such trial shall be held in the State where the said crime shall have been committed; but when not-committed within any State, the trial shall be at such place or places as the Congress may by law have directed.

SECTION III.

1. Treason against the Confederate States shall consist only in levying war against them, or in adhering to their enemies, giving them aid and comfort. No person shall be convicted of treason, unless on the testimony of two witnesses to the same overt act, or on confession in open court.

2. The Congress shall have power to declare the punishment of treason, but no attainder of treason shall work corruption of blood, or forfeiture, except during the life of the person attainted.

ARTICLE IV.

SECTION I.

1. Full faith and credit shall be given in each State to the public acts, records and judicial proceedings of every other State. And the Congress may, by general laws, prescribe the manner in which the such acts, records and proceedings shall be proved, and the effect thereof.

SECTION II.

1. The citizens of each State shall be entitled to all the privileges and immunities of citizens in the several States, and shall have the right of transit and sojourn in any State of the Confederacy, with their slaves and other property; and the right of property in said slaves shall not be thereby impaired.

2. A person charged in any State with treason, felony, or other crime against the laws of such State, shall, on the demand of the Executive authority of the State from which he fled, be delivered up to be removed to the State having jurisdiction of the crime.

3. No slave, or other person held to service or labor, in any

State or Territory of the Confederate States, under the laws thereof, escaping or lawfully carried into another, shall, in consequence of any law or regulation therein, be discharged from such service or labor; but shall be delivered up on claim of the party to whom such slave belongs, or to whom such labor or service may be due.

SECTION III.

1. Other States may be admitted into this Confederacy by a vote of two-thirds of the whole House of Representatives, and two-thirds of the Senate, the Senate voting by States; but no new State shall be formed or erected within the jurisdiction of any other State; nor any State be formed by the junction of two or more States, or parts of States, without the consent of the Legislatures of the States concerned, as well as of the Congress.
2. The Congress shall have power to dispose of and make all needful rules and regulations concerning the property of the Confederate States, including the lands thereof.
3. The Confederate States may acquire new territory; and Congress shall have power to legislate and provide governments for the inhabitants of all territory belonging to the Confederate States, lying without the limits of the several States; and may permit them, at such times, and in such manner, as it may by law provide, to form States to be admitted into the Confederacy. In all such territory, the institution of negro slavery, as it now exists in the Confederate States, shall be recognized and protected by Congress, and by the Territorial Government; and the inhabitants of the several Confederate States and Territories shall have the right to take to such Territory any slaves, lawfully held by them in any of the States or Territories of the Confederate States.
4. The Confederate States shall guarantee to every State that is or hereafter may become a member of this Confederacy, a republican form of government, and shall protect each of them against invasion; and on application of the Legislature, (or of the Executive, when the Legislature is in session,) against domestic violence.

ARTICLE V.

SECTION I.

1. Upon the demand of any three States, legally assembled in their several conventions, the Congress shall summon a convention of all the States, to take into consideration such amendments to the Constitution as the said States all concur in suggesting at the time when the said demand is made; and should any of the proposed amendments to the Constitution be agreed on by the said convention—voting by States—and the same be ratified by the Legislatures of two-thirds of the several States, or by conventions

in two-thirds thereof—as the one or the other mode of ratification may be proposed by the general convention—they shall thenceforward form a part of this Constitution. But no State shall, without its consent, be deprived of its equal representation in the Senate.

ARTICLE VI.

1. The Government established by this Constitution is the successor of the Provisional Government of the Confederate States of America; and all the laws passed by the latter shall continue in force until the same shall be repealed or modified; and all the officers appointed by the same shall remain in office until their successors are appointed and qualified, or the offices abolished.

2. All debts contracted, and engagements entered into, before the adoption of this Constitution, shall be as valid against the Confederate States under this Constitution as under the Provisional Government.

3. This Constitution, and the laws of the Confederate States, made in pursuance thereof, and all treaties made, or which shall be made, under the authority of the Confederate States, shall be the supreme law of the land; and the judges in every State shall be bound thereby, anything in the Constitution or laws of any State to the contrary notwithstanding.

4. The Senators and Representatives before mentioned, and the members of the several State Legislatures, and all executive and judicial officers, both of the Confederate States and of the several States, shall be bound by oath or affirmation to support this Constitution; but no religious test shall ever be required as a qualification to any office of public trust under the Confederate States.

5. The enumeration, in the Constitution, of certain rights shall not be construed to deny or disparage others retained by the people of the several States.

6. The powers not delegated to the Confederate States by the Constitution, nor prohibited by it to the States, are reserved to the States, respectively, or to the people thereof.

ARTICLE VII.

1. The ratification of the Convention of five States shall be sufficient for the establishment of this Constitution between the States so ratifying the same.

2. When five States shall have ratified this Constitution in the manner before specified, the Congress under the Provisional Constitutional shall prescribe the time for holding the election of President and Vice-President, and for the meeting of the Electoral College, and for counting the votes, and inaugurating the President. They shall, also, prescribe the time for holding the first election of members of Congress under this Constitution, and the

time for assembling the same. Until the assembling of such Congress the Congress under the provisional constitution shall continue to exercise the legislative powers granted them; not extending beyond the time limited by the Constitution of the Provisional Government.
Adopted, unanimously, March 11, 1861.

CONFEDERATE STATES.

The organization of the Confederate States Government commenced under a Provisional Constitution on the 8th day of February, 1861, and expired on the 18th day of February, 1862. Jefferson Davis, of Mississippi, and Alexander H. Stephens, of Georgia, were chosen as President and Vice President for the Provisional term of one year.

The first Presidential term of six years under the permanent Constitution commenced on the 22d of February, 1862, and will expire on the 18th day of February, 1868.

The First election for President and Vice President under the permanent Constitution took place on the 6th day of November, 1861, in each State of the Confederacy.

Total number of States voting..11
Total number of electoral votes cast........................109
Of which number Jefferson Davis, of Mississippi, received for the office of President of the Confederate States...........109
Alexander H. Stephens, of Georgia, received for the office of Vice-President of the Confederate States..................109

The number of electoral votes cast by the several States is as follows:

	Representation in Congress.	Votes.
Virginia	16	18
North Carolina	10	12
South Carolina	6	8
Georgia	10	12
Florida	9	4
Alabama	9	11
Louisiana	6	8
Texas	6	8
Arkansas	4	6
Mississippi	7	9
Tennessee	11	13
	87	109

SALARIES OF THE EXECUTIVE OFFICERS.

President..........................$25,000 per year
Vice-President..................... 6,000 "
Secretary of State................. 6,000 "
"   Treasury.................. 6,000 "
"   War....................... 6,000 "
"   Navy...................... 6,000 "
Attorney-General................... 6,000 "
Postmaster-General................. 6,000 "

The salary of members of Congress shall be eight dollars per day during the session. Each member shall be allowed ten cents per mile for coming to, and ten cents for returning from, the place where Congress may assemble for each session. The salary of the President of Congress shall be sixteen dollars per day, and the mileage as same as members.

The President and Vice-President are elected for a term of six years, and are not re-eligible to office. The Senate is composed of two members from each State in the Confederacy, chosen by the Legislatures of each State, for six years. The Senate is divided into three classes, and one-third of their number are chosen every two years. The members of the House of Representatives are elected by the people for a term of two years. Congress assembles once in every year, commencing on the 18th day of February.

GOVERNMENT OF THE CONFEDERATE STATES.

Jefferson Davis, of Mississippi, President.
Alexander H. Stephens, of Georgia, Vice-President.

THE CABINET.

J. P. Benjamin, of Louisiana, Secretary of State.
C. G. Memminger, of South Carolina, Secretary of Treasury.
James A. Seddon, of Virginia, Secretary of War.
S. R. Mallory, of Florida, Secretary of Navy.
Thomas H. Watts, of Alabama, Attorney-General.
J. H. Reagan, of Texas, Postmaster-General.

FIRST CONGRESS OF THE CONFEDERATE STATES.

SENATE.

Alabama—†Clement C. Clay, †William L. Yancey.
Arkansas—†Robt. W. Johnson, Charles B. Mitchell.
Florida—James M. Baker, †Augustus E. Maxwell.
Georgia—Benjamin H. Hill, †Robert Toombs.
Kentucky—†Henry C. Burnett, †William E. Simms.
Louisiana—Thomas J. Semmes, Edward Sparrow.
Mississippi—†Albert G. Brown, James Phelan.

AND REPOSITORY OF USEFUL KNOWLEDGE. 33

Missouri—†John B. Clark, R. S. T. Peyton.
North Carolina—George Davis, William T. Dortch.
South Carolina—†Robt. W. Barnwell, †James L. Orr.
Tennessee—Langdon C. Haynes, Gustavus A. Henry.
Texas—William S. Oldham, †Louis T. Wigfall.
Virginia—Robert M. O. T. Hunter, Wm. Ballard Preston.

Those having the † prefixed have served in the United States Congress. The number of old Congressmen in the Senate will be fourteen. New Congressmen, twelve. Total, twenty-six.

HOUSE OF REPRESENTATIVES.

Dist. ALABAMA.
1. Thomas J. Foster.
2. †William R. Smith.
3. John P. Ralls.
4. †J. L. M. Curry.
5. †Francis S. Lyon.
6. Wm. P. Chilton.
7. †David Clopton.
8. †James L. Pugh.
9. †Edw. L. Dargan.

ARKANSAS.
1. Felix I. Batson.
2. Grandison D. Royston.
3. Augustus H. Garland.
4. Thomas B. Hanly.

FLORIDA.
1. James B. Dawkins.
2. Robert B. Hilton.

GEORGIA.
1. Julian Hartridge.
2. C. J. Munnerlyn.
3. Hines Holt.
4. Augustus H. Kenan
5. David W. Lewis.
6. William W. Clark.
7. †Robert P. Trippe.
8. †Lucius J. Gartrell.
9. Hardy Strickland.
10. †Augustus R. Wright.

KENTUCKY.
1. Alfred Boyd.
2. John W. Crockett.
3. H. E. Read.
4. Geo. W. Ewing.
5. †James S. Chrisman.
6. T. L. Burnett.

Dist. MISSOURI.
3. Casper W. Bell.
4. A. H. Conrow.
5. George G. Vest.
6. Thomas W. Freeman.
7. John Hyer.

NORTH CAROLINA.
1. †W. N. H. Smith.
2. Robert R. Bridgers.
3. Owen R. Keenan.
4. T. D. McDowell.
5. Thomas S. Ashe.
6. Arch. H. Arrington.
7. Robert McLean.
8. William Lander.
9. B. S. Gaither.
10. A. T. Davidson.

SOUTH CAROLINA.
1. †John McQueen.
2. †W. Porcher Miles.
3. L. M. Ayer.
4. †Milledge L. Bonham.
5. James Farrow.
6. Wm. W. Boyce.

TENNESSEE.
1. Joseph T. Heiskell.
2. William G. Swan.
3. W. H. Tebbs.
4. E. L. Gardenshire.
5. †Henry S. Foote.
6. †Meredith P. Gentry.
7. †George W. Jones.
8. Thomas Menees.
9. †J. D. C. Atkins.
10. †John V. Wright.
11. David M. Currin.

7. H. W. Bruce.
8. S. S. Scott.
9. E. M. Bruce.
10. J. W. Moore.
11. Robt. J. Breckinridge.
12. John M. Elliott.

LOUISIANA.
1. Charles J. Villere.
2. †Charles M. Conrad.
3. Duncan F. Keener.
4. Lucien J. Dupre.
5. John F. Lewis.
6. †John Perkins, Jr.

MISSISSIPPI.
1. J. W. Clapp.
2. †Reuben Davis.
3. Israel Welch.
4. H. C. Chambers.
5. †O. R. Singleton.
6. E. Barksdale.
7. †John J. McRae.

MISSOURI.
1. W. M. Cook.
2. Thomas A. Harris.

TEXAS.
1. †John A. Wilcox.
2. C. C. Herbert.
3. Peter W. Gray.
4. B. F. Sexton.
5. M. D. Graham.
6. Wm. B. Wright.

VIRGINIA.
1. †M. R. H. Garnett.
2. John R. Chambliss.
3. James Lyon.
4. †Roger A. Pryor.
5. †Thomas S. Bocock.
6. John Goode, Jr.
7. J. P. Holcombe.
8. †D. C. DeJarnett.
9. †William Smith.
10. †A. R. Boteler.
11. John R. Baldwin.
12. Walter R. Staples.
13. Walter Preston.
14. Albert G. Jenkins.
15. Robert Johnston.
16. Charles W. Russell.

Those marked with the † have been members of the United States Congress. The number of old Congressmen will be thirty-three. New Congressmen, seventy-two.

SENATORIAL TERMS.

Alabama—Mr. Clay, 2 years; Mr. Yancey, 6 years.
Arkansas—Mr. Johnson, 2 years, Mr. Mitchell, 6 years.
Florida—Mr. Baker, 2 years; Mr. Maxwell, 4 years.
Georgia—Mr. Toombs, 2 years; Mr. Hill, 6 years.
Kentucky—Mr. Simms, 2 years; Mr. Burnett, 6 years.
Louisiana—Mr. Semmes, 4 years; Mr. Sparrow, 6 years.
Mississippi—Mr. Phelan, 2 years; Mr. Brown, 4 years.
Missouri—Mr. Clarke, 2 years; Mr. Peyton, 4 years.
North Carolina—Mr. Davis, 2 years; Mr. Dortsch, 4 years.
South Carolina—Mr. Barnwell, 4 years; Mr. Orr, 6 years.
Tennessee—Mr. Henry, 4 years; Mr. Haines, 6 years.
Texas—Mr. Wigfall, 4 years; Mr. Oldham, 6 years.
Virginia—Mr. Preston, 4 years; Mr. Hunter, 6 years.

OUR INDIAN RELATIONS.

The information which has been furnished Congress by the report communicated to that body by the Indian Bureau, in reference to the condition of the Indian country, is of an interesting nature. The fact is disclosed that a very large majority of the Indians are true to the Government of the Confederate States, and are as orderly in their conduct, and as obedient to the requirements of the law, as ever before. Disaffection, however, exists among the Cherokees, Creeks and Seminoles, and perhaps the small bands of Osages, Quapaws, &c., who live upon the borders of Kansas, within easy reach of the machinations and baneful influences of the enemy, have become generally disloyal. In regard to this, however, nothing is certainly known, as no information from the Osage agency is in the 'possession of the bureau.' The disaffection among the Cherokees seems to be of a limited extent, and among the Creeks and Seminoles, although a short time ago it had taken rather a wide range, (having reached a large portion of both tribes,) has been counteracted in a great degree, it is hoped by the defeat of Ho-poi-iph-li Yo-ho-lo, and the arrival of General Pike in the country.

Within the four great tribes—the Choctaws and Chickasaws, Creeks, Seminoles and Cherokees—the hostilities pending between the Confederate and the Northern States, have interfered with agricultural and mechanical pursuits, and the success of schools. The military spirit moving certain portions of these people, and the want of the money which has heretofore been paid them by the old United States Government, have been the causes of this derangement in their industrial and educational operations.

The report of the government contains an interesting statement of the geographical features of the country inhabited by the tribes of red men who have linked their fortunes with those of the Confederate States.

The Indian Territory (not including the Osage country—its extent being unknown—nor the 800,000 acres belonging to the Cherokees, which lie between Missouri and Kansas,) embraces an area of 82,073 square miles—more than fifty-two and a half millions of acres, to wit:

The land of the Cherokees, Osages, Quapaws, Senecas, and Shawnees, 28,105 square miles, or 24,288,800 acres;

That of the Creeks and Seminoles 20,581 square miles, or 13,140,000 acres;

That of the Reserve Indians, and the Choctaws and Chickasaws, 23,437 square miles or 15,000,000 acres;

Total 82,073 square miles, or 52,528,800 acres.

Its population consists of Cherokees, 23,000; Osages, 7,500; Quapaws, 320; Creeks, 13,500; Seminoles, 2,500; Reserve Indians, 2,000; Choctaws, 17,500, and Chiickasaws, 4,700—making an aggregate of 71,520 souls.

This Indian country is, in many respects, really a magnificent one. It is one of the brightest and fairest spots of the great West. By the hand of nature it has been blessed with advantages in great profusion, and of the highest and rarest character. Diversified by mountains filled with iron, coal and other mineral treasures, and broad reaching plains capable of grazing, for a large portion of the year, innumerable herds of cattle—with the Red river running along its southern border, the Arkansas river almost through its centre, and their tributaries reticulating its entire surface—possessed of a climate generally mild and genial, and a soil unsurpassed for depth and fertility, adapted to the growth of cotton; hemp and all kinds of grain, it is certainly the equal naturally of the most favored lands on this continent, and only needs the development of its resources to become an invaluable adjunct of the Confederate States.

PRODUCTION OF BREADSTUFFS—STATISTICS FROM THE CENSUS OF 1860.

The following statistics are derived from the last United States census reports:

WHEAT, RYE AND CORN PRODUCED IN THE UNITED STATES IN 1860.

States,	Wheat. Bushels.	Rye. Bushels.	Corn. Bushels.
California	5,946,600	55,000	524,800
Connecticut	52,400	618,700	2,059,800
Delaware	913,000	27,200	3,892,400
Illinois	24,159,500	981,200	115,396,800
Indiana	15,219,100	400,200	69,641,600
Iowa	8,433,200	176,000	41,117,000
Kansas	168,500	3,900	5,678,800
Kentucky	7,394,800	1,055,300	64,043,600
Maine	233,900	123,300	1,546,000
Maryland	6,103,500	519,000	13,445,000
Massachusetts	119,800	388,000	2,115,000
Michigan	8,313,200	494,200	12,552,100
Minnesota	2,195,800	124,300	2,685,600
Missouri	4,227,600	598,300	72,892,000
New Hampshire	239,000	128,300	1,414,700
New Jersey	1,763,100	1,489,500	9,723,300
New York	8,681,100	4,787,000	20,961,000
Ohio	14,532,000	656,100	70,637,100
Oregon	822,400	2,700	74,600
Pennsylvania	13,045,200	5,474,800	28,796,800
Rhode Island	1,100	28,300	459,000
Vermont	431,100	131,000	6,463,000
Wisconsin	15,812,600	887,500	7,565,300
Territories	1,007,400	11,200	2,767,200
Total bushels	139,816,500	18,803,100	549,786,700

AND REPOSITORY OF USEFUL KNOWLEDGE.

Seceding States.	Wheat.	Rye.	Corn.
Alabama	1,222,500	74,000	32,761,200
Arkansas	955,300	77,900	17,758,700
Florida	2,800	21,300	2,824,500
Georgia	2,545,000	115,600	80,776,300
Louisiana	29,300	12,800	16,205,900
Mississippi	579,500	41,300	29,563,700
North Carolina	4,743,700	436,800	80,078,600
South Carolina	1,285,600	89,100	15,065,600
Tennessee	5,409,000	260,300	50,748,300
Texas	1,464,300	95,000	16,521,600
Virginia	13,169,160	944,000	38,360,700
Seceding States	31,367,000	2,173,100	280,655,100
Other States	139,816,500	18,803,100	549,736,700
Totals, 1860	171,183,500	20,976,200	830,451,800
" 1850	100.486,000	14,188,800	592,071,000

The relative value of these three products in the loyal and in the seceding States may be represented as follows:

	Wheat at $1.25.	Rye at 75c.	Corn at 50c.
Loyal States	$174,770,000	$14,103,000	$274,893,000
Seceding States	39,209,000	1,630,000	140,332,000
Total, 1860	$213,979,000	$15,733,000	$415,225,000
" -1850	125,607,000	10,641,600	296,025,000

From this official return it would appear that New York, which was in 1830–40, one of the leading wheat producing States, has now become the seventh, and is about on a parallel with Michigan in the article of wheat. Agriculturists state that the cultivation of wheat or any other article for a long series of years, without intermission, is an injury to the soil and to the crops. If New York would recover her position as a leading State in the production of wheat, more attention must be given to rotation of crops. The relative position of this State as a wheat producer, since 1840, is shown in the annexed summary of all the States producing over five million bushels each.

WHEAT-PRODUCING STATES, 1840, 1860.

	1840.	1850.	1860.
Illinois,	3,335,400	9,414,600	24,159,500
Indiana,	4,049,400	6,214,400	15,219,100
Wisconsin,	212,100	4,286,100	15,812,600
Ohio,	16,571,600	14,487,300	14,532,600
Virginia,	10,109,700	11,212,600	13,129,100
Pennsylvania,	13,213,000	15,367,700	13,045,200
New York,	12,286,400	13,121,500	8,681,100
Michigan,	2,157,100	4,925,800	8,313,200
Iowa,	151,700	1,530,500	8,433,200
Kentucky,	4,803,100	2,142,800	7,394,800
Maryland,	3,345,700	4,494,600	6,103,500
California,		17,200	2,946,600
Tennessee,	4,569,700	1,619,400	5,469,900
Thirteen States,	74,804,900	88,834,500	146,180,400
All others,	13,708,300	11,651,300	25,003,100
Bushels of Wheat,	88,513,200	100,485,800	171,183,500

Thus the West and Northwest must become the future granary for the supply of the Eastern States of Europe, while other States, giving more attention to other crops, neglect the cereals.

New York, in 1840, with a population of 2,428,921, produced 12,286,400 bushels of wheat, or five bushels *per capita*, and in 1850 a little over four bushels *per capita;* but now this production is reduced to about two and a quarter bushels each. The production of the whole country per head, according to the census of 1840-1860, has been as follows:

Year.	Population.	Wheat. Product.	Bushels. per Capita.
1840,	17,069,453	88,513,000	5.12
1850,	23,191,876	100,485,000	4.33
1860,	31,445,089	171,183,000	5.44

Of the facilities for increased production in the United States, the new report of the Superintendent of the Census, says:

"Whether the superior agricultural advantages and the demand for the implements and machinery in the United States have stimulated the facile ingenuity of our mechanics, or have only been seconded by its ready contributions to industry, we shall not stop to inquire. The greatest triumphs of mechanical skill in its application to agriculture are witnessed in the instruments adapted to the tillage, harvesting and subsequent handling of the immense grain crop of the country, and particularly upon the western prairies. Without the improvements in ploughs and other implements of tillage, which have been multiplied to an incredible extent, and are now apparently about to culminate in the steam plough, the vast wheat and corn crops of those fertile plains could not probably be raised. But were it possible to produce wheat upon the scale it is now raised, much of the profits and not a little of the product would be lost were the farmer compelled to wait upon the slow process of the sickle, the cradle and the hand rake for securing it when ripe, The reaping machine, the harvester, and machines for threshing, winnowing and cleaning his wheat for the market, have become quite indispensable to every large grain grower. The commercial importance of the wheat crop, and its various relations to the subject of domestic and foreign supply, to markets, the means of transportation, storage, &c., make it highly important that the producer shall have the means of putting his crop in the market at the earliest or most favorable time and with the greatest precision.

While the surplus of the year, 1860, must have been large, there is no doubt that the production in 1861 and 1862 has been much larger, probably exceeding two hundred millions of bushels of wheat. It is well to recur, in the consideration of this question, to the returns of foreign exports from the United States in breadstuffs. These were officially stated as follows:

Year.	Value.	Year.	Value.
1845	$7,445,000	1853	$21,875,000
1846	16,605,000	1854	48,383,000
1847	58,262,000	1855	21,557,000
1848	22,608,000	1856	56,619,000
1849	22,896,000	1857	55,624,000
1850	13,066,000	1858	33,698,000
1851	14,556,000	1859	24,893,000
1852	17,256,000	1860	28,590,000

In the year 1861 the value of breadstuffs and provisions exported had increased to $94,866,000, against $45,271,000 in the previous year. These facts show conclusively that the United States are capable of producing wheat and corn to such an extent as will enable us to become a creditor nation in our trade with European countries. The gold of the Pacific, the breadstuffs of the West and Northwest, added to a protective tariff, will, together, contribute to reinstate public credit and individual enterprise whenever the end of the war shall arrive.

DOMESTIC AND INDIAN MISSIONS.

We have received a copy of the seventeenth annual report of the Board of Directors of Domestic and Indian Missions of the Southern Baptist Convention, from which it appears that the receipts for the Domestic department have been $5,389.85, and the disbursements $4,511.52, leaving with the amount on hand at the opening of the year—$1,673.63—a balance in the treasury of $3,652.03. The receipts in the Indian department were $8,606.88, and the disbursements for the same time, $9,505.90. The report contains interesting reports of the operations of the Board, in the different fields of labor.

THE "VALUE" OF THE LATE UNITED STATES.

The census of 1860 shows the following as the money value of the "glorious" but defunct Union:

States.	Assessed value of Real Estate.	Assessed value of Personal Estate.	True Value of Real and Personal Estate.
Maine,	$86,717,716	$67,662,672	$190,211,600
New Hampshire	59,638,346	64,171,743	156,310,860
Vermont	65,039,973	19,118,646	122,477,170
Massachusetts	475,413,165	301,744,651	815,237,433
Rhode Island	83,778,204	41,326,101	135,337,588
Connecticut	191,478,842	149,778,134	444,274,114
New York	1,069,658,080	320,806,558	1,843,338,517
New Jersey	151,161,742	145,520,550	467,918,324
Pennsylvania	561,192,980	158,060,355	1,416,501,818
Delaware	26,273,803	13,493,430	46,242,181
Maryland	65,341,438	231,793,800	376,949,944
Virginia	417,952,228	239,069,100	793,249,681
North Carolina	116,366,573	175,931,029	358,739,399
Florida	21,722,810	47,206,875	73,101,500
Alabama	155,034,089	277,164,673	495,237,078
Louisiana	280,704,988	155,082,277	602,118,568
Arkansas	63,254,740	116,956,590	219,256,472
D. Columbia	33,097,542	7,987,403	41,084,945
Missouri	153,430,577	118,485,274	501,214,398
Kentucky	277,925,054	250,287,639	666,043,112
South Carolina	129,772,684	359,546,444	548,138,754
Illinois	287,219,940	101,987,432	871,860,282
Indiana	201,829,992	119,112,482	528,835,371
Texas	112,476,013	155,316,322	365,200,614
Kansas	16,088,602	6,429,630	31,327,895
Iowa	149,433,423	55,733,560	274,338,265
Tennessee	219,991,180	162,504,020	493,903,892
Michigan	123,605,084	39,927,921	257,163,983
Wisconsin	148,238,766	37,706,723	273,671,668
California	66,906,631	72,748,036	207,874,613
Minnesota	25,391,771	6,727,001	52,294,413
Ohio	687,518,121	272,348,980	1,193,898,422
Mississippi	157,836,737	351,636,175	607,324,911
Georgia	179,801,441	438,430,946	645,895,237
Oregon	6,279,602	12,745,313	28,930,637
New Mexico	7,018,260	13,828,520	20,813,768
Utah	286,504	3,861,516	5,596,118
Washington	1,876,063	2,518,672	5,601,466
Nebraska	5,732,145	1,694,804	9,131,056
			$16,159,916,086

LIABILITIES OF THE CONFEDERATE STATES.

STATEMENT FOR THE YEAR ENDING SEPTEMBER 1ST, 1862.

The present liabilities of the Southern Confederacy are said to approximate to the following figures:

Borrowed from Banks	$50,000,000
State aid, to be reimbursed	45,000,000
Due bills for property seized	65,000,000
Due bills for property destroyed	40,000,000
War loans	65,000,000
Treasury notes	100,000,000
Due soldiers	45,000,000
Total	$410,000,000

COTTON AND SUGAR.

The New Orleans Shipping List has been resumed. The cotton statement shows a beggarly account. The stock on the 20th of August was 352 bales. The receipts during the year, ending September 1st, were 39,730 bales. Exported for the year, 27,296 bales. The statistics of the sugar crop of Louisiana are as follows:

The actual yield is estimated to have comprised 459,410 hogsheads, averaging 1,150 lbs. and making an aggregate weight of 528,231,500 pounds. This embraced 389.264 hogsheahs of brown sugar, made by the old process, and 70,146 refined, clarified, etc., including cistern bottoms, the whole being the product of 1,291 sugar-houses, of which 1,027 were worked by steam and 264 by horse power. The crop of the preceding year amounted to 228,753 hogsheads, weighing 263,065,000 lbs., showing an increase for the last year of 263,065,000 lbs., showing an increase for the last year of 230,657 hogsheads, or 265,266,500 pounds.

According to our calculations the price of the entire crop has averaged 4¾c. against 5½c. last year. At this average, and taking the estimate of 1,150 pounds to the hogshead, the aggregate value of the crop of 459,410 hogsheads is $25,095,291, against $14,468,627, the product of 228,753 hogsheads last year; or an increase of $10,626,644. The receipts on the levee since the 1st of September have been 225,356 hogsheads, and 7,907 tierces and barrels, against 174,637 hogsheads and 5,976 tierces and barrels last year.

The stock now on hand in the State is estimated at 170,000 hogsheads.

The yield of molasses from the last year's cane crop is estimated at 70 gallons for each 1,000 pounds of sugar, against the same for the previous year, or an aggregate of 36,982,505 gallons against 18,414,550 the year previous, showing an increase of 18,567,955 gallons, or more than as much again. The arrivals at the levee during the season have been 401,404 barrels, against 313,260 last year, showing an increase of 87,944 barrels.

The total value of the product, estimated at an average of 18¼ cents per gallon, sums up $6,703,079 against $4,235,446 last year, showing an increase of $2,467,733.

STATE GOVERNMENTS OF THE CONFEDERATE STATES.

States.	Capitals.	Governors.	Term Expires.	Salary.	Legislature Meets.	General Election.
Alabama	Montgomery.	J. G. Shorter.	December, 1863.	$4000	2d Monday Nov.	1st Monday Aug.
Arkansas	Little Rock.	H. Flanagan.	November, 1864.	2500	1st Monday Nov.	1st Thurs. Sept.
Georgia	Milledgeville.	Jos. E. Brown.	November, 1863.	4000	1st Monday Nov.	1st Monday Oct.
Louisiana	Baton Rouge.	Thos. O. Moore	January, 1864.	4000	3d Monday Jan.	1st Monday Nov.
Mississippi	Jackson.	John J. Pettus.	November, 1863.	4000	1st Monday Nov.	1st Monday Oct.
North Carolina	Raleigh.	C. B. Vance.	January, 1864.	3000	3d Monday Nov.	1st Thurs. Aug.
South Carolina	Columbia.	F. W. Pickens.	December, 1862.	3800	4th Monday Nov.	2d Monday Oct.
Tennessee	Nashville.	I. G. Harris.	October, 1863.	3000	1st Monday Oct.	1st Thurs. Aug.
Texas	Austin.	F. R. Lubbock.	December, 1864.	3000	1st Monday Nov.	1st Monday Aug.
Virginia	Richmond.	John Letcher.	January, 1864.	5000	1st Monday Dec.	4th Thurs. May.
Florida	Tallahassee.	John Milton.	October, 1865.	2500	4th Monday Nov.	1st Monday Oct.
Missouri	Jefferson City.	C. F. Jackson.	December, 1864.	3000	1st December.	1st Monday Aug.

POPULATION OF THE CONFEDERATE STATES,
ACCORDING TO THE CENSUS OF 1860.

States.	White.	Slaves.	Total.
Virginia	1,097,373	495,826	1,593,100
North Carolina	697,965	328,377	1,008,342
South Carolina	308,186	407,185	715,371
Georgia	615,336	467,461	1,082,797
Florida	81,865	93,809	145,694
Alabama	520,444	435,473	935,917
Mississippi	407,551	497,607	887,158
Louisiana	354,245	312,186	666,431
Arkansas	331,710	109,065	440,775
Texas	515,999	184,956	600,955
Tennesse	859,528	287,112	1,146,640
Missouri	1,185,590	115,619	1,301,209
Kentucky	920,077	225,490	1,145,567
	7,895,869	3,960,166	11,669,956

POPULATION OF THE TERRITORIES.

Territories.	Population in 1850.	Population in 1860.
New Mexico	61,547	93,024
Arizona		9,000

RATES OF POSTAGE IN THE CONFEDERATE STATES OF AMERICA.

RATES OF POSTAGE BETWEEN PLACES WITHIN THE CONFEDERATE STATES OF AMERICA.—*On Letters.*—Single letters, not exceeding half an ounce in weight, for any distance 10 cents; an additional single rate for each additional half ounce or less. Drop letters, 2 cents each. In the foregoing cases, the postage to be prepaid by ssamps or stamped envelopes. Advertised letters, 2 cents each.

On Packages—Containing other than printed or written matter —money packages are included in this class—to be rated by weight, as letters are rated, and to be charged the same rate of postage as on letters, to wit: For any distance, ten cents for each half ounce or less. In all cases to be prepaid by stamps or stamped envelopes.

On *Newspapers* sent to regular and *bona fide* subscribers from the office of publication, and not exceeding 3 ounces in weight :
Within the State where Published.—Weekly paper, 6¼ cents per

AND REPOSITORY OF USEFUL KNOWLEDGE. 45

quarter; semi-weekly paper, 13 cents per quarter; tri-weekly paper, 19½ cents per quarter; daily paper, 39 cents per quarter. In all cases the postage to be paid quarterly in advance, at the offices of the subscribers.

Without the State where Published.—Weekly paper, 13 cents per quarter; semi-weekly paper, 26 cents per quarter; tri-weekly paper, 39 cents per quarter; daily paper, 78 cents per quarter. In all cases the postage to be paid quarterly in advance at the offices of the subscribers.

On Periodicals sent to regular and *bona fide* subscribers from the office of publication, and not exceeding 1½ ounce in weight:

Within the State where Published.—Monthly, 3 cents per quarter, or 1 cent for each number; semi-monthly, 6 cents per quarter, or 1 cent for each number—an additional cent each number for every additional ounce or less beyond the first 1½ ounce; bi-monthly, or quarterly, 1 cent an ounce. In all cases the postage to be paid quarterly in advance at the offices of subscribers.

Without the State where Published.—Not exceeding 1½ ounce in weight:

Monthly, 6 cents per quarter, or 2 cents for each number; semi-monthly, 12 cents per quarter, or 2 cents for each number—two cents additional for every additional ounce or less beyond the first 1½ ounce; bi-monthly, or quarterly, 2 cents an ounce. In all cases the postage to be paid quarterly in advance, at the office of the subscribers.

On Transient Printed Matter.—Every other newspaper, pamphlet, periodical and magazine, each circular not sealed, handbill and engraving, not exceeding three ounces in weight, 2 cents, for any distance—two cents additional for each additional ounce or less beyond the first 3 ounces. In all cases the postage to be prepaid by stamps or stamped envelopes.

Franking Privilege.—The following persons only are entitled to the franking privilege, and in all cases strictly confined to official business: Postmaster-General, his Chief Clerk, Auditor of the Treasury for the Post-office Department, and Deputy Postmasters, the Chiefs of Contract and Finance Bureaus.

POPULATION OF SOME OF THE PRINCIPAL CITIES IN THE SOUTHERN STATES.

CITIES.	STATES.	1850	1860
Baltimore	Maryland.	169,054	212,418
New Orleans	Louisiana	116,375	172,786
St. Louis	Missouri	77,860	160,479
Louisville	Kentucky	43,194	75,196
Charleston	South Carolina	37,989	48,494
Richmond	Virginia	27,570	39,860
Savannah	Georgia	15,312	28,789
Mobile	Alabama	20,515	24,720
Nashville	Tennessee	18,478	29,783
Memphis	Tennessee	10,841	29,830
Montgomery	Alabama	8,728	12,243
Augusta	Georgia	8,225	16,490
Natchez	Mississippi	4,439	7,321
Petersburg	Virginia	14,610	18,213
Norfolk	Virginia	14,336	18,965
Wilmington	North Carolina	7,268	12,362
Galveston	Texas	5,210	10,112
Vicksburg	Mississippi	4,740	7,420

The number of Volunteer troops raised in some of the States, previous to the enforcement of the Conscription act, were:

  Alabama .... 65,000 men
  South Carolina .... 41,873 "
  Georgia .... 33,000 "

PATENT OFFICE REPORT.

The Report of the Commissioner of Patents, which has been sent into Congress, shows the following as the condition of the office at the close of the past year:

  Number of applications for Patents 304
  do Caveats 110
  do Patents issued 57
  do United States Patents and Assignments thereof recorded 112
  Amount of Fees received $9,000 90
  Amount of expenditures 6,188 28

  Excess of receipts over expenditures .. $2,812 62

The considerable excess of the receipts over the expenditures, up to the period to which this report extends, and which has resulted in placing a surplus of $2,812 ¢2 in the Treasury to the credit of the Patent Fund, sufficiently demonstrates that the office is the most prosperous in its financial department, and that it is self-sustaining.

A COMPARATIVE VIEW OF THE SOUTHERN AND NORTHERN TRADE, &c.

There is so much misapprehension in relation to our foreign trade, and it is so important at the present juncture to have a correct understanding upon the subject, that at the risk of repetition, we shall recur to it again. For this purpose we shall take from the official returns of 1861 the amount of exports, distinguishing the exclusively Northern from the exclusively Southern origin of of the articles:

UNITED STATES EXPORTS.

Northern origin.	Southern origin.
	Forest $6,085.931
Products of the sea. $4,156,180	Breadstuffs 9,567.397
Forrest 9,368,917	Cotton 191,800,755
Provisions 20,215,226	Tobacco 19,278,621
Breadstuffs 19,022,901	Hemp, etc. 746,870
Manufactures 25,599,547	Manufactures 10,934,795
Northern origin... $77,363,070	Southern origin... $238,419,680

Total exports........................... $335,782,740
Imports consumed....................... 336,380,172

These are the figures of the Treasury table, and their careful consideration may dispel some strange illusions that possess the public mind. Among the items, it will be observed, under the head of products of the forest, Georgia pine and lumber, naval stores, etc., bear a high figure. All those who have been patiently awaiting the South to be "starved out," will observe with some surprise that it supplies one-third of all the breadstuffs exported from the Union. Hence, if they cannot eat cotton, they will not starve. The manufactures which originate in the South form also a small sum total for which many are not prepared.

The result is, that the North furnishes one-fourth of the merchandise exported and the South three-fourths. It will now be understood that three-fourths of the national exports are embargoed by blockade. It is very important thoroughly to understand that fact, because on it hangs all the finance of the war. Breadstuffs and provisions, it will be observed, form one-half of the Northern exports, and the harvest in England being good, those articles, if sold at all, must be sold very low.

If we turn to the importations into the country we find the following results:

IMPORTS.

	Specie.	Goods.	Total.
North	$4,780,598	$316,842,381	$321,592,970
South	3,770.546	36,802,738	40,573,284
Total	$8,551,135	$353,645,119	$362,166,254

The specie imports at the South are mostly silver from Mexico, and of the merchandise, coffee counts $9,731,617; sugar for $3,500,000; for Western account, iron, queens-ware, etc., for the balance. Now, if we bring the aggregates together, they will show as follows:

	Total Im.	Total Ex.	Excess Im.	Excess Ex.
North	$316,812,381	$77,367,070	$239,449,311	
South	36,802,738	238,419,670		$201,616,932

We have here the conclusive fact that the three fourths of the whole foreign trade of the country is Southern. The exports are produced there, and the goods they get payment for come to them through New York to the great profit of its merchants. The South also sent North for Northern consumption in 1860, as follows:

Cotton, 1,000,000 bales............$55,000,000
Tobacco,........................... 10,000,000
Sugar.............................. 18,000,000
Rice............................... 1,000,000
Wheat and Corn..................... 5,000,000
Naval Stores....................... 1,000,000

Total..........$90,000,000

In this connection, we call attention to the following from the London Economist, in relation to the British trade for the first three months of this year:

"Our commerce with the South and with the North is now for the first time divided in the official tables. It appears that all our direct exports are to the North. The figures are:

Exports to Northern States, — — £3,922,133
Exports to Southern States, — — 174,563

Showing a startling contrast in the amount we actually sell to to the two belligerents. The contrast is nearly as remarkable in what we buy, only it is reversed!—

Imports into Great Britain from Northern ports, £4,697,868
Imports into Great Britain from Southern ports, 6,786,186

"We see in these simple figures the record of the causes of much that has occurred in Lombard street.

"It is therefore difficult to say with which of the combatants in this struggle we are the most connected. One party supplies us with the materials of our industry, the other party purchases the fruits of that industry from us."

This is a very singular error for so high a commercial authority as the London Economist to fall into. What England receives is Southern produce, direct from the South: but what she sends to the North, that is to say, New York, is on its way to the South. When the separation takes place England would not continue to sell largely to the North, but the goods would go direct fo the ports from whence the raw material is derived. In such a state or affairs, the West would be bound over hand and foot to the Eastern States. She would have to buy their manufactures dear and sell them food cheap. The interests of the South and the West are identical, both being agricultural, and both of them sources of supply for Europe in opposition to the Eastern States. The great Western valley of the Mississippi, with its undeveloped natural manufacturing advantages, has the vast Southern market open to its future enterprise, when capital shall have accumulated from agricultural industry and fertile land. This war is retarding her progress fifty years at least, and perhaps ruining it forever.

THE CONDITION OF BANKS IN THE SOUTHERN STATES FOR 1860.

The report of the Secretary of the Treasury of the United States of March 26, 1860, gives a statement of the condition of the banks of the Southern States, from which we have prepared the following tables, showing their capital, loans and discounts, specie, circulation and deposits:

Southern States.	No. Banks and Branches	Capital.	Loans and Discounts	Specie	Circulation	Deposits
Alabama	8	$4,901,000	$13,570,027	$2,747,174	$7,477,976	$4,851,153
Delaware	12	1,640,775	3,150,215	208,924	1,135,772	976,226
Florida	2	300,000	464,630	32,876	183,640	129,518
Georgia	29	16,689,560	16,776,282	3,211,974	8,798,100	4,738,289
Kentucky	45	12,835,670	25,284,869	4,502,250	13,520,207	5,662,892
Louisiana	13	24,496,866	35,401,609	12,115,431	11,579,313	19,777,312
Maryland	31	12,568,962	20,898,762	2,779,418	4,106,869	8,874,180
Missouri	38	9,082,951	15,461,192	4,169,212	7,884,885	3,357,176
North Carolina	30	6,626,478	12,213,272	1,617,687	5,594,047	1,487,273
South Carolina	20	14,962,062	27,801,912	2,324,121	11,475,634	4,165,615
Tennessee	34	8,067,037	11,751,019	2,267,710	5,538,378	4,324,799
Virginia	65	16,205,156	24,975,792	2,943,652	9,812,197	7,720,652
Texas						
Arkansas						
Mississippi						
New Mexico & Ind'n Ter'y						
Total	327	$128,176,517	$207,749,681	$38,912,129	$87,107,018	$66,074,585

AND REPOSITORY OF USEFUL KNOWLEDGE. 51

THE POSTMASTER-GENERAL'S REPORT.

The total cost of the mail service in the eleven States of Alabama, Arkansas, Florida, Georgia, Louisiana, Mississippi; North Carolina, South Carolina, Tennessee, Texas and Virginia, for the fiscal year ending June 30th, 1860, under the Government of the United States, was 4,296,246.78; and the total receipts for postal service, for the same year, were $1,517,540.55. Excess of expenditures over receipts, $2,778,706.23. The receipts for the fractional quarter of one month, ending the 30th of June last has shown by the meagre and imperfect returns) were $92,387.97, and the expenditures $200,937.97; excess of expenditures over receipts, $108,553.30.

Of an appropriation of $30,000 to carry into effect an Act of Congress, "relative to telegraph lines in the Confederate States," there has been expended $15,136.77. Eight lines of telegraph have been built, of the aggregate length of 217 miles, at an aggregate cost of $4,365.32. Ten and a half miles of insulated copper wire, with batteries, &c., have been made and sent to the army for field operations, at a cost of $4,763.86. Operators and watchmen have been employed at a cost of $1,696.22, of which $1,513.70 has been paid. Contracts were made with the Texas Telegraph Company and with the Arkansas State Telegraph Company for building and operating lines, and sending Government dispatches to distant portions of the Confederacy. The first was to have been completed by the 10th of December.

There are in the Confederate States 2579 post roads established by law, Of these, contracts have been prepared in duplicate, and sent in letters of instruction to Postmasters for execution by the contractors on 1872 routes, and 883 of the number have been returned properly executed.

There are 91 railroads and branch roads in the Confederate States; of this number only 15 have entered into contracts. tracts. Many of the companies have waived the proposal to contract for the present, on one or another ground. Many of them decline to accept the classification and compensation assigned to their roads, and intend, if they can, to avoid liability and the legitimate control of the Department by refusing to enter into contracts, while, at the same time, they signify a willingness to perform the service, but under some protest, and generally that they must have higher pay.

The whole number of Postoffices in the Confederate States on the 1st of June, 1861, was 8,411. Of this number there have been discontinued since that date, 183, leaving in operation 8228; number established since the 1st of June, 72; whole number now in in operation, 8300. Number of postoffices, of which the names and sites were changed, 47; number of postmasters appointed since the 1st of June, 6261; number commissioned by the Department since that date, 4184; whole number of resignations during the same period, 950, of which number 459 were resignations of appointments conferred by this Department, and 491 were resignations of appointments held under the Government of the United States. There are 110 route agents employed. Seven permanent and one temporary special agents have been appointed.

Estimate of the probable receipts for the year ending June 30, 1862, compared with the receipts from all the postoffices now in the Confederate States for the fiscal year ending June 30, 1860:

Total receipts of all the offices in 1860............$1,517,536 00
Total receipts of all the offices in 1861............ 1,091,012 00

Showing a deficiency of..........................$426,524 00

This estimate, however, is based upon the returns from only 2,922 postoffices, and the receipts must necessarily be increased by the returns from the remaining 4,024, though the latter are generally small offices, scattered throughout the interior, from many of which the receipts will be inconsiderable.

THE FINANCIAL CONDITION OF THE CONFEDERACY:

From Richmond Examiner.

We are enabled from papers before Congress to prepare a succinct and interesting statement of the financial condition of the country, and to enlighten the public as to the amount of our public debt; its classes; the receipts of the Treasury up to 1st August; and the probable demands that will be made upon the resources of the South in view of the continuance of the war and the exigencies of the country arising therefrom. We distribute this information under appropriate heads;

THE PUBLIC DEBT OF THE CONFEDERACY.

It is ascertained from official data, furnished by the Treasury Department, that the whole expenditures of the Government from the commencement to the 1st of August last, amount to $347,272,958.85. It should be stated, however, that five millions of the amount charged as expenditure, has been paid for the redemption of deposit certificates, and the aggregate above stated is subject to that abatement when considered in the light of actual expenses.

The expenditures up to the first of August are as follows:

War Department......................$298,376,549 41
Navy Department.................... 14,005,777 86
Civil and Miscellaneous.............. 15,766,503 48

$328,748,830 70

AND REPOSITORY OF USEFUL KNOWLEDGE.   53

To which must be added outstanding requisitions upon the Treasury, upon which warrants are not yet issued, to the amount of $18,524,128 15; making the aggregate, as stated above, $347,272,958.85.

CLASSES OF THE PUBLIC DEBT.

An examination of our funded debt account will show that a lamentably small portion of our public debt exists in this form. The whole amount of bonds and stock issued is as follows:

Eight per cent. stock and bonds................$41,577,250
Six   "   call certificates................. 32,784,400
                                                 ───────────
                                                 $74,361,650

This statement indicates an evident indisposition of our people to make investments in this form, and furnishes an explanation of much of that disturbance of the standard of value and enhancement of prices in the country, which have been the consequence of the large and disproportionate issue of Treasury notes.

The issue already made of Treasury Notes amounts to $183,244,135; leaving authority to issue $16,756,865.

RECEIPTS AT THE TREASURY.

The receipts at the Treasury up to 1st August from all the various sources of income are as follows:

From Customs... $1,437,399 96
"   Miscellaneous sources................................. 1,974,769 33
"   Loan, act of Feb. 28th, 1861........................ 15,000,000 00
"   "   "   Aug. 19th, 1861....................... 22,613,346 61
"   Call Deposits under act of December 24, 1861......... 37,585,200 00
"   Treasury Notes, act March 9th, 1861.................. 2,021,100 00
"   "   "   act May 16, 1861..................... 17,347,955 00
"   "   "   act Aug. 19, 1861....................167,764,615 00
"   Int. "   " act April 17, 1861.................. 22,977,900 00
" $1 & 2 " 846,000 00
"   Temporary Loan from Banks—balance................... 2,625,000 00
"   War Tax... 10,539,910 70
                                                         ──────────────
                                                         $302,555,196 60

This statement of receipts is short of the whole amount of the expenditures of the Government by $44,717,762; on account of which the Government has authority to issue only the balance of Treasury Notes $16,755,165, leaving $27,961,897 to be provided for by Congress in a further extension of the general currency, unless this balance can be paid by bonds or otherwise.

FUNDS TO BE RAISED BY THE FIRST OF JANUARY.

It is supposed that the authority to issue general currency notes

must also be extended by Congress to meet the appropriations already made by it and not yet paid, and also the further appropriations to be made.
The appropriations already made by Congress, and not drawn on 1st of August, amount to... $164,687,339 93
The estimates submitted by the various Departments of the additional supplies required to make good deficiencies and to support the Government to 1st January next, are as follows:
For the War Department................................$44,373,590 36
" Civil List.. 386,607 39
" Miscellaneous.................................... 102,899 38
                                                  ─────────────
                                                  $44,863,091 13
So that the whole amount of supplies required to 1st January presents a total of................$209,550,487 06
Congress is left to determine the best mode of raising this sum, and as there seems but little prospect of raising the money by a sale of bonds or stock, a resort to Treasury notes seems to be all that will be left to its discretion.

INTEREST BEARING NOTES.

The experiment of diminishing the quantity of circulation by interest-bearing notes and deposits on call, is said to have been very successful, and is likely to be enlarged as a relief from excess in the quality of the national currency, which, as it exceeds the usual business wants of the community, must be productive of high prices without relation to the *actual value* of the currency.

It is understood that the interest notes, although current to a certain degree, have been generally withdrawn from circulation, on account of their value as temporary investments. Most of them have been taken under the belief that the interest would be paid like other interest, and the Secretary of the Treasury has encouraged this belief by a recommendation to Congress that the interest should be paid annually.

PROSPECTS OF ANOTHER WAR TAX—PAYMENT BY THE STATES, &C.

It is supposed that Congress will be under the necessity of providing another tax. From the war tax returns and from estimates as to such States as have not yet made complete returns, this fund may be set down at seven hundred millions.

The War Tax has been paid by the several States as follows:
North Carolina..$1,400,000 00
Virginia... 2,125,000 00
Louisiana.. 2,500,000 00
Alabama.. 2,000,000 00
Georgia,... 434,126 12
Florida.. 225,374 11
Mississippi.. 1,484,467 67
                                                          ─────────────
                                                          $10,168,967 90

The State of Georgia has substantially paid in the balance due by her, and the State of South Carolina has paid the whole amount due by her into the Treasury, in the form of six per cent. call certificates. But as the final settlement has not yet taken place, the certificates have not as yet been delivered up, and the account is not yet closed. The returns from the States of Alabama, Louisiana, Mississippi, Arkansas and Texas have not yet been rendered in complete. The two former States have, nevertheless, paid their taxes in advance.

LOUISIANA AND ALABAMA STATE FINANCE—
FINANCES AND PROGRESS.

The whole debt of Louisiana on the first day of January last was composed of the following items:

Bonds for Citizens' Bank	$4,297,333 33	
Bonds for Consolidated Association	1,101,200 00	
		$5,398,533 33
Railroad subscriptions:		
Jackson Railroad	$884,000	
Opelousas Railroad	641,000	
Vicksburg and Shreveport	260,000	
Grosse Tete	70,000	
		1,855,000 00
The Railroad Debts:		
Old Nashville Bonds	$483,000	
Mexican Gulf Railroad	100,000	
Port Hudson and Clinton	9,000	
		592,000 00
Old Second Municipality	$198,240	
Charity Hospital	125,000	
		323,240 00
Juvenile School Fund	$529,000	
Seminary Fund	136,000	
		665,000 00
For relief of Treasury		750,000 00
Whole Bond Debt		$9,583,773 33
There are Trust Funds for which the State is liable, payable on demand, amounting to		575,300 99
Making the whole State debt about		$10,159,074 32

The total receipts into the Treasury of Louisiana last year, including receipts on account of trust funds, were $2,378,793 44; the expenditures, $2,224,702 10.

The taxable property of Louisiana has increased within ten years from $265,000,000 at which it was assessed in 1850 and 1851, to $420,000,000, at which it was assessed in 1860—an increase of $150,000,000. The rate has averaged about $15,000,000 per annum, but it has been quite irregular; 1853 was assessed at nearly $30,000,000 over 1852, and 1856 $37,000,000 over 1855, while the estimated excess of 1860 over 1859 is only $4,000,000. The increase has, however, been constant. if not uniform.

ALABAMA.

The bond debt of our State is $3,445—annual interest $185,820. The domestic debt is $2,582,178, most of which draws interest, being the sixteenth section and University fund, etc. The Legislature has just authorized the issue of $2,000,000 in bonds, the issue of $1,000,000 in Treasury notes, and has loaned the Southern Congress $500,000. The balance in the Treasury on the 1st of January last was $298,668; nett revenue during the present year estimated at $847,000—total of means, $1,172,669. Past appropriations due, $600,650; due educational fund, $285,000; State expenses, $200,000—total, $1,058,650. Total balance estimated to be in the Treasury at the close of the present year, $266,274. The expenses of the present military preparations of the State are not taken into the above estimates. They are expected to be met out of the new issue of the State bonds and the issue of Treasury notes. There was no increase of taxes by the last Legislature, although the expenditures were largely increased.

NORTH CAROLINA AND ARKANSAS STATE FINANCES AND RESOURCES.

The assessed value of real estate in North Carolina in 1815 was $58,521,513; in 1836 this value had actually decreased, and in 1850, thirty-five years later, it had only increased to $55,600,000; but in 1860 it reaches $126,000,000, or $76,400,000 more than 1850. This result, the Governor believes, comes solely from the internal improvements, which only fairly commenced in 1850.

The public debt of the State is $9,129,505. To this is to be added $4,699,900, for which the public faith is pledged to certain railroads. Of this latter sum, about $1,500,000 will be required within two years. The expenditures of the two next years are estimated at $728.424.76, to meet which the estimate of receipts is $1,726,425.06. It is therefore evident, not only that there need be no increase of taxes, but that they may be reduced.

AND REPOSITORY OF USEFUL KNOWLEDGE. 57

To meet the principal of her liabilities, the State has, in stocks and bonds of various railroads, canals and sinking fund, $7,633,140. The sinking fund, from which the public debt is to be paid, and which is made up of dividends of stock owned by the State, and any accruing balances, now amounts to $457,040, and for the last two years has received $419,570. After this year, the Governor estimates that the annual addition to this fund will be not less than a million of dollars, to come from railroad dividends. He relies upon the roads being profitable, because having been built by slave abor, their cost is very much less than Northern roads.

DEBT OF ARKANSAS.

The payment of the State debt, up to October 1st, 1840, amounted to $2,341,996.17.. The amount of outstanding debt on account of the Bank of the State of Arkansas is $1,098,717.50, and the liability of the State for bonds sold by the Real Estate Bank, and interest due on them, was $1,654,825.28 on the 1st of October. There is beside an additional liability for principal and interest up to the 1st day of October, 1860, $267,455.71 on account of the $121,336.50 borrowed by the bank on the 7th September, 1840, upon the five hundred bonds of the State, which the bank, in violation of law, hypothecated to the "North American Trust and Banking Company," of New York. This company sold the bonds and placed them beyond the control of the State.

The State, the Governor says, has made considerable progress in getting out of debt, and in a few years will be entirely so. The whole value of property taxed in the State in the year 1852 was $42,000,000, and the increase during the subsequent eight years amounted to about $1,000,000. There remained in the Treasury on the 1st of October for ordinary expenses $304,106 in gold and silver. An appropriation of $130,000 out of the five per cent. accruing from the sales of public lands is recommended for the completion of the Memphis and Little Rock Railroad, and of the Mississippi, Ouachita and Red River Railroad. The attention of the Legislature is also called to the subject of public education.

DEBT AND RESOURCES OF THE STATE OF VIRGINIA.

The receipts for the fiscal year ending September 30th, 1863, including the balance on hand at the commencement of that year, amounted to $1,899,634.36. There was expended that year the sum of $1,895,002.23; leaving a balance in the treasury on the 1st October, 1860, of $4,632.13.

The receipts for the fiscal year ending Sept. 30th, 1861, including the balance on hand at the commencement of that year amounted to $1,775,091,72. There was disbursed during the same period the sum of $1,766,871.29; leaving a balance on hand 1st of October, 1861, of $8,220.43.

The investments of the fund in stocks, loans, &c., other than subscriptions and appropriations to internal improvements, amount in the aggregate to $5,108,483.33.

The amount of bonds of corporations, the payment of the interest and the principal of which is guaranteed by the Commonwealth, is $2,035,805. The amount heretofore reported was 3,898,500. Since the last regular session of the Legislature, under an act passed 23d March, 1860, $1,862,695 of the guaranteed bonds of the James River and Kanawha Company have been converted into State bonds. The interest due the 1st day of July last on the bonds of the Chesapeake and Ohio Canal Company, guaranteed by the State, has not been paid, no report having been made by that company of its inability to pay the interest.

The amount appropriated by State subscriptions to joint stock companies, and for State improvements, upon which payments have been made, is $40,642,189.88, and the amount paid is $35,508,266.71, leaving a balance of $5,133,923.47 yet to be paid; which, added to $9,600, the amount of subscriptions to companies now authorized, on which no payments have been made, makes the sum of $5,143,523.17.

The amount authorized to be subscribed to companies of whose organization no information has been received, is $385,740, which added to the aggregate amount of the two items last stated, makes $5,529,263.17, and constitutes a contingent liability of the Commonwealth.

Estimates are given of certain and probable receipts on account of the revenue of the fund of Internal Improvement for the fiscal years ending 30th September, 1862, and 30th September, 1863, after deducting the estimated charges for the same. The surplus for the year 1862 is supposed to be $238,750.39; and that for 1863, $258,759.39.

The amount paid out of the Sinking Fund on account of the redemption of certificates of public debt issued prior to 1st January, 1852, in the two years 1860 and 1861, is $462,688.31, and the amount paid for certificates of public debt purchased for an investment for said fund in the two years, is $581,012.11.

The aggregate outstanding debt, consisting of registered and coupon bonds in the hands of the public and the Commissioners of the Sinking Fund on the 30th September, 1861, is ascertained to be $34,806,824.32. The net increase of the public debt, during the last two fiscal years, is $4,619,507.69; which increase includes guaranteed bonds of the James River and Kanawha Company changed to State bonds, ($1,862,695,) armory expenditures, ($164,500,) and subscriptions to railroad and other improvement companies.

AND REPOSITORY OF USEFUL KNOWLEDGE. 59

The amount of public debt issued prior to 1st January, 1852, and now outstanding, is $10,271,107.99, and is called the old debt— that created since the 1st of January, 1862, amounts to $24,538,- 716.38, and is called the new debt. The Commissioners of the Sinking Fund have advertised to redeem, on the 31st December, $60,614.96 of the above public debt.

The aggregate amount of the funds and resources of the Commonwealth is $43,080,704.19; of which amount $8,120,805.99 are productive of a revenue equivalent to about four and one-half per cent. The remainder or unproductive portion consists of bonds and loans, which are more or less available and secured by mortgages, &c., and stocks in improvements not completed, and also in improvements completed which yield no dividend.

HOG STATISTICS.

The following comparative statement of the number of hogs raised in all the States and Territories in 1850, shows that the slave States raised 20,715,835, against $9,601,439 in the free States and Territories combined. These statistics, it will be observed, were compiled previous to the secession of Missouri and Kentucky:

NUMBER OF HOGS IN THE SOUTHERN CONFEDERACY.

Virginia	$1,830,743
North Carolina	1,812,813
South Carolina	1,065,503
Georgia	2,168,617
Florida	299,543
Alabama	1,904,540
Mississippi	1,582,734
Louisiana	597,301
Texas	684,514
Arkansas	836,727
Tennessee	3,104,800
Total	15,796,835

DOUBTFUL BORDER STATES.

Maryland	352,911
District of Columbia	1,635
Kentucky	2,861,163
Missouri	1,702,625
Total	4,918,334
Total number of hogs raised in all the old United States in 1850	30,316,608

By this it appears that in 1850 there were in the
Confederate States............................15,796,835
Doubtful Border States, (Maryland, Kentucky, Missouri,
  Delaware and District of Columbia.............. 4,918,334

All the Slave States................................20,715,885
Free States and Territories........................ 9,602,439

  Balance in favor of Slave States.................11,118,780

RAILROADS IN THE SOUTH.

The following tables from data given in the Railroad Journal, and the published returns of the late census, showing the miles of railroad in operation in each State, and their cost with equipments, and the area of territory of each State:

SOUTHERN STATES.	Miles of Railroad in operation.	Cost, with equipment.	Area, in sq. miles.
Alabama....................	798.6	$20,975,639	50,772
Arkansas...................	38.5	1,130,110	52,198
Delaware...................	47.9	2,345,825	2,120
Florida....................	289.8	6,368,699	59,268
Georgia....................	1,241.7	25,687,220	58,000
Kentucky...................	458.5	13,852,062	37,680
Louisiana..................	419.0	16,073,270	41,346
Maryland and Dist. of Columbia.	833.3	41,526,424	11,070
Mississippi................	365.4	9,024,444	47,151
Missouri...................	723.2	31,771,116	65,037
North Carolina.............	770.2	13,698,469	45,500
South Carolina.............	807.3	19,083,343	34,000
Tennessee..................	1,062.3	27,348,141	44,000
Texas......................	284.5	7,578,943	274,357
Virginia...................	1,525.7	43,069,360	61,352
New Mexico and Indian Territory			400,000
Totals.....................	9,665.0	$279,533,065	1,283,850

AND REPOSITORY OF USEFUL KNOWLEDGE. 61

CENSUS OF 1860.

States.	Whites.	Slaves.	Total.
Alabama	529,164	435,132	964,296
Arkansas	324,324	111,104	435,427
California	380,015		380,015
Connecticut	460,151		460,151
Delaware	110,420	1,798	112,218
Florida	78,686	61,753	140,439
Georgia	595,097	462,230	1,057,327
Illinois	1,711,753		1,711,753
Indiana	1,350,479		1,350,479
Iowa	674,948		674,948
Kansas	107,110		107,110
Kentucky	930,223	225,490	1,155,713
Louisiana	376,913	332,523	709,433
Maine	628,276		628,276
Maryland	599,846	87,188	687,034
Massachusetts	1,231,065		1,231,065
Mississippi	354,699	436,696	791,395
Missouri	1,058,352	114,555	1,173,817
Michigan	749,112		749,112
Minnessota	162,022		162,022
New Hampshire	326,972		326,072
New Jersey	672,031		672,031
New York	3,887,542		3,887,542
North Carolina	661,586	331,081	992,667
Ohio	2,339,599		2,339,599
Oregon	52,464		52,464
Pennsylvania	2,906,370		2,906,370
Rhode Island	174,621		174,621
South Carolina	301.271	402,541	703,812
Tennessee	834,063	275,784	1,109,847
Texas	420,651	180,388	601,039
Vermont	315,116		315,116
Virginia	1,105,196	490,887	1,596,083
Wisconsin	775,873		775,873
Population of States,	27,185,109	3,949,557	31,134,666

CENSUS OF 1860.

TERRITORIES.	CENSUS OF 1860.		
	Whites.	Slaves.	Total.
Population of States............	27,185,109	3,949,557	31,134,666
Colorado......................	34,197		84,197
Dakotah.......................	4.839		4,839
Nebraska......................	28,832	10	28,842
Nevada........................	6,587		6,857
New Mexico....................	93,517	24	93,541
Utah..........................	40,266	29	40,295
Washington....................	11,578		11,578
District of Columbia..........	71,895	3,181	75,076
Total Population..............	27,477,090	3,962,801	31,429,891

COTTON SUPPLY AND CONSUMPTION OF EUROPE.

The following table shows the Import, Consumption and Stocks in the whole of Europe for the years 1859 and 1860, and is compiled from the Annual Report of Messrs. Stolterfoht, Sons & Co., Liverpool:

```
                                1860.                    1859.
Stock, Jan. 1, bales...        571,000                 557,000
Import to 31st Dec....
  Great Britain......3,638,000               2,829,000
  France............  685,000                  436,000
  Continent (direct)..  479,000—4,532,000    588,000—3,853,000

Total supply........           5,103,000                4,410,000
Do. Stock, Dec. 31...            782,000                  571,000

Delivered for cons'n..         4,321,000                3,829,000
Sources of Supply.
  Confederate States..3,648,000              3,030,000—3,803,000
  Brazil.............  106,000                 130,000
  West Indies........   47,000                  30,000
  East Indies........  573,000                 514,000
  Egypt.............1,580,000—4,532,000      149,000—3,853,000
```

The whole Cotton crop of the Confederate States in 1860 was 4,697,926 bales. The total exports of cotton for the same year was 4,625,725 bales. Of this amount England received 2,254,400 bales.

The whole crop for the year 1861 was 3,699,926 bales. The total exports to foreign ports for the same year was 3,764,341 bales. Of this amount England received 1,998,467 bales. England derives a revenue of $350,000,000 per annum from American cotton.

The cotton fields of the Southern States embrace an area of 500,000 square miles, and the capital invested in the cultivation of the plant amounts to $900,000,000. Seventy years ago, the exports of our cotton were only 420 bales—not one-tenth of the amount furnished by several countries to England. Now, the South furnishes five-sevenths of the surplus cotton product of the entire world.

PLACES AND TIMES OF HOLDING THE CIRCUIT COURTS IN THE CONFEDERATE STATES OF AMERICA.

ALABAMA, Mobile, 2d Monday in April and 4th Mon. in Dec.
ARKANSAS, Little Rock, 2d Monday in April.
GEORGIA, N. Dist., Marietta, 2d Monday in March and Sept.
GEORGIA, S. Dist., Savannah, 2d Mon. in April—Milledgevillle, Thursday after 1st Monday in November.
KENTUCKY, Frankfort, 3d Monday in May and October.
LOUISIANA, New Orleans, 4th Mon. in April and 1st Mon. in November.
MISSISSIPPI, Jackson, 1st Monday in May and November.
MISSOURI, St. Louis, 1st Monday in April and (special) Oct.
NORTH CAROLINA, Raleigh, first Monday in June and last Monday in Nov.
SOUTH CAROLINA, Charleston, first Monday in April;—Columbia, 4th Monday in November.
TENNESSEE, M. Dist., Nashville, 3d Mon. in April and Oct.
TENNESSEE, E. Dist., Knoxville, 3d Monday in May and 4th Monday in November.
TENNESSEE, W. Dist., Jackson, first Mon. in April and Oct.
VIRGINIA, E. Dist., Richmond, first Monday in May and fourth Monday in November.
VIRGINIA, W. Dist., Lewisburg, first Monday in August.

PLACES AND TIMES OF HOLDING THE DISTRICT COURTS.

ALABAMA, N. Dist., Huntsville, second Monday in May and November.
ALABAMA, M. Dist., Montgomery, fourth Monday in May and November.
ALABAMA, S. Dist., Mobile, fourth Monday in April and second Monday after 4th Monday in November.

ARKANSAS, E. Dist., Little Rock, first Monday in April and October.
ARKANSAS, W. Dist., second Monday in May and November.
FLORIDA, N. Dist., Tallahassee, 1st Monday in January, Apalachicola, first Monday in February; Pensacola, first Monday in March; St. Augustine, first Monday in April.
FLORIDA, S. Dist., Key West, first Monday in May and Nov.
GEORGIA, N. Dist., Marietta, second Monday in March and September.
GEORGIA, S. Dist., Savannah, second Tuesday in February, May, August and November.
KENTUCKY, Frankfort, third Monday in May and October.
LOUISIANA, E. Dist., New Orleans, third Monday in February, May and November.
LOUISIANA, W. Dist., Opelousas, 1st Monday in August; Alexandria, first Monday in September; Shreveport, 1st Monday in October; Monroe, 1st Monday in November; St. Joseph, 1st Monday in December.
MISSISSIPPI, N. Dist., Pontotoc, first Monday in June and December.
MISSISSIPPI, S. Dist., Jackson, fourth Monday in January and June.
MISSOURI, E. Dist., St. Louis, third Monday in February, May and November.
MISSOURI, W. Dist., Jefferson City, first Monday in March and September.
NORTH CAROLINA, Edenton, third Monday in April and Oct; Newbern, fourth Monday in April and October; Wilmington, first Monday after fourth Monday in April and October.
SOUTH CAROLINA, E. Dist., Charleston, first Monday in January, May, July and October.
SOUTH CAROLINA, W. Dist., Greenville Court House, first Monday in August.
TENNESSEE, E. Dist., Knoxville, third Monday in May and fourth Monday in November.
TENNESSEE, M. Dist., Nashville, third Monday in April and October.
TEXAS, E. Dist., Galveston, first Monday in May and December; Brownsville, first Monday in March and October.
TEXAS, W. Dist., Austin, first Monday in January and June; Tyler, fourth Monday in April and first Monday in November.
VIRGINIA, E. Dist., Richmond, 12th May and 12th November; Norfolk, 30th May and 1st November.
VIRGINIA, W. Dist., Staunton, first May and first October; Wythe Court House, fourth Monday in May and October; Charleston, 19th April and 19th September; Clarksburg, 24th March and 24th August; Wheeling, 6th April and 6th September.

SOME OF THE PRINCIPAL COLLEGES AND PROFESSIONAL SCHOOLS IN THE CONFEDERACY.

NAME.	PLACE.	Vols. in Lib'y	Commencement of Session.
Southern University.	Greensboro, Ala.		
University of North Carolina.	Chapel Hill, N. C.	21,000	First Thursday in June.
Franklin.	Athens, Ga.	18,250	First Wednesday in August
South Carolina.	Columbia, S. C.	24,000	First Monday in December.
University of Alabama.	Tuscaloosa, Ala.	12,000	First Thursday in July.
University of Louisiana.	New Orleans, La	5,300	Last Thursday in July.
Centenary College.	Jackson, La.		July.
Mississippi College.	Clinton, Miss.	3,750	Last Thursday in July.
Howard	Marion, Ala.	3,000	Last Thursday in June.
Mercer University.	Penfield, Geo.	8,700	Fourth Wednesday in July
Oglethorpe.	Milledgeville, Geo.	18,250	First Wednesday in Aug.
Davidson.	Mecklenburg, N. C.	21,000	First Thursday in June.
University of Virginia.	Charlottesville, Va.	30,000	June 29th.
Randolph Macon.	Boydon, Va.	8,000	Fourth Thursday in June.
University of Nashville.	Nashville, Tenn.	9,666	Last Thursday in June.
University of Mississippi.	Oxford, Miss.	550	Not in session at present.
Semple Broaddus.	Centre Hill, Miss.		Last Thursday in July.
Dolbear's Commercial.	New Orleans, La.		Constantly in session.
East Tennessee.	Knoxville, Tenn.	8,000	First Wednesday in July,
Transylvania.	Lexington, Ky.	14,000	Last Thursday in June.
Union.	Murfreesboro, Tenn.	4,300	First Wednesday in July.
Medical College of Alabama.	Mobile.		
St. Louis.	St. Louis, Mo.	2,2000	

DIARY OF THE WAR FOR SEPARATION.

(*Continued from C. S. Almanac, for* 1862.)

1862.

January 1. Engagement at Fort Pickens. The Federals, in command at Fort Pickens, opened fire on a Confederate vessel in the bay. Col. Anderson, being in command of the Confederates, promptly opened his batteries on Fort Pickens. The firing lasted nearly half a day. No casualties reported by the Confederates.

Battle near Port Royal river, South Carolina. The Federals advanced up Port Royal river and gave battle to the Confederates, after a brisk fight the Federals driven back defeated. Federal loss 17 killed 9 wounded. Confederate loss 8 killed 15 wounded.

January 4. Judge Hemphill, of Texas, died in Richmond, Va.

January 5. Skirmish at Hanging Rock, near Romney, Va. Confederate loss, 5 killed and 7 captured.

January 6. French man-of-war approached Ship Island under a neutral flag for the purpose of business with the French Consul at New Orleans, and was fired into by the Federal vessel. An apology soon made.

January 8. Skirmish on Silver Creek, Mo. Confederates defeated.

January 9. Col. Lubbock, of the Texas Rangers, died. Burnside expedition left Annapolis.

January 10. Battle of Middle Creek, near Prestonburg, Ky. The Confederate forces under Gen. Humphrey Marshall was attacked by the Federals. The Federals severely defeated. Gen. Marshall in his official report says:

"My loss in the action of the 10th inst., is accurately stated at 10 killed and 14 wounded. The loss of the enemy was severe, estimated by the officers of my command, who had an opportunity to see them dead, at over 200 killed and more than that wounded. The enemy had some 4,500 or 5,000 men on the field, and at least 500 cavalry (for that number was counted.) I had some 1,600 men fit for duty and present on the field. He engaged probably 2,500 or 3,000 of his men; I about 900 or 1,000 of mine."..... Senators Johnson and Polk, of Mo., expelled from U. S. Senate, charged with treason to the Government.

January 12-13. Burnside expedition left Old Point, and caught in a succession of damaging storms before reaching Hatteras.

January 14. Secretary Cameron, of the Lincoln Cabinet, resigns, and is succeeded by Stanton, of Pa., as Secretary of War.

January 15. The Federal gun boats made an attack on Fort Henry, Tennessee river, and retired without doing any damage to the Fort.

January 16. Battle near Ironton, Mo. Confederate troops under Jeff. Thompson, drove the enemy towards Pilot Knob.

January 17. Ex-President Tyler, died in Richmond, Va.

January 19. Battle at Fishing Creek, or Mill Springs, Ky. The Confederate forces, under command of Gen. Crittenden and Zollicoffer, advances from their entrenchments and attack the Federals under Gens. Thomas and Schoepf. The Confederates were repulsed and Gen. Zollicoffer killed. His death is thus described:

Soon after the fight began, not far from the entrenchments of the enemy on Sunday morning, Gen. Zollicoffer mistook a regiment of Kentuckians for one of his own command. He rode up very near the Colonel. The first intimation he had of his position was received when it was too late. "There's old Zollicoffer," cried out several of the regiment in front of him. "Kill him!" and in an instant their pieces were leveled at his person. At that moment Henry M. Fogg, aid to Gen. Zollicoffer, drew his revolver and fired, killing the person who first recognized Gen. Z. With the most perfect coolness, Gen. Z. approached to the head of the enemy, and drawing his sabre cut the head of the Lincoln Colonel from his shoulders. As soon as done, twenty bullets pierced the body of our gallant leader, and Gen. Zollicoffer fell from his horse a mangled corps.

The Confederate force engaged was only 4,700 while the Federals numbered 14,000. Confederate loss was 114 killed, 102 wounded and 45 taken prisoners. Federal loss, 92 killed, 194 wounded.

January 22. A brisk skirmish took place near Boston, Ky. The Federals were badly whipped and lost 8 killed and 5 wounded. Confederate loss, 3 wounded.

January 27. Reported fight at James Island, Fla. Sixty

Federals reported killed and 35 captured. Confederate loss, 13 killed and wounded.

January 29. Reported skirmish near Occoquan, Va. Nine Texans killed and 1 wounded..... Naval engagement near Fort Pulaski, Ga. No lives lost.

January 30. The state of affairs in the North is thus described:

The most candid of the Northern people confessed their disappointment, especially with reference to two topics—the integrity of the slave population and the tremendous amount of resistance the South has offered to the resources and best exertions of the North. Expressions opposing the prosecution of the war were every day becoming more open and more careless of restraint. It was commonly said that the Democratic party would soon be in power again in the North, and that its programme would be to upset the whole present system of Yankee government and deal terrible vengeance upon those responsible for the consequences of the war. We are told that public expressions were more than once heard that "Cameron and Welles should be hung," and that the work of retribution should go on until "every man who had loaned money to the government had been treated to a halter." Regrets, at once pitiful and ridiculous, were lavished on the destruction of "the Union."

The resignation of Cameron, Lincoln's Secretary of War, was treated with congratulations by the less ultra people of the North; and it was said that Welles' resignation would soon follow. The "emancipationists" were excessively annoyed, and were showing the most infamous exasperation of feeling. The pages of Harper's Weekly were adorned with scurrilous cuts and illustrations given of an exasperated policy of conquest, in pictures of Southern ladies "of the first families" delving at wash tubs under Massachusetts task masters.

There was a general feeling of despair at the financial aspects of the war. It was stated, on authority, that no more specie would be paid out of the Federal Treasury except for interests on the old public debt. The financial programme at Washington was understood to be an additional issue of demand notes to the amount of a hundred and fifty to two hundred millions of dollars, and a war tax to the amount of a hundred and fifty millions; although it was estimated in well-informed quarters that the increased expenses of the war would run up to $1,000,000,000 a year. All private loans had ceased, and the full coming of crisis was awaited in a sort of dreary despair. The newspapers were endeavoring to animate confidence, but the influence of the press in the North—owing to its long course of deception in the war—had positively expired.

February 1. Skirmish at Bloomery, Western Va. A large party of Federals surprised and captured 45 Confederates. The Federals lost 15 killed and wounded. The Federals elated with their success, committed great outrages on the inhabitants of the neighborhood.

February 4–5–6. Attack and capture of Fort Henry, Tennessee river. The Fort was attacked by Federal gun boats, and a force of 10,000 men under Gen. Grant. Gen. Tilghman made a brave defence, but was forced to surrender before an overwhelming force; two gun boats were badly damaged. Confederate loss was 10 killed, 13 wounded, and Gen. Tilghman with 57 men were taken prisoners. Gen. Heiman with 3,000 men succeeded in making a safe retreat to Fort Donelson. Federal loss 45 killed, (32 scalded to death on one gun boat) and 60 wounded..... Santa Fe, New Mexico, evacuated by the Federals who retreated to Fort Union..... Sixty Federal war vessels appeared at Roanoke Island, North Carolina.

February 7–8. The Federal gun boats ascend the Tennessee river to Florence, Ala., creating great excitement among the people living along the river. Several Confederate Steamboats were burned and destroyed to prevent their falling into the hands of the enemy. The Federals seized on a quantity of Confederate stores at Florence; after committing many depredations, the Federals returned with their boats to Paducah.... Battle of Roanoke Island, North Carolina. The Federals landed 10,000 men and attacks the Confederate batteries and captured the Island. Capt. O. J. Wise was killed and 2,437 Confederates taken prisoners. Our entire loss is but 23 killed, and some 58 wounded, while that confessed to by the foe, and reported to us by one of the party, who accompanied Capt. Wise's body home. was 35 commissioned officers, including two colonels, and 175 privates killed, and between 300 and 400 wounded. This fact attests more strongly than language could do, the heroism of the defense. Let the battle of Roanoke Island be classed no longer among the disasters of the war ; rather let us cherish the memory of the deeds that there ennobled our arms, and shed fresh lustre upon the brilliant historic fame of the Southern volunteers. The enemy admit 300 killed and wounded, while our estimate of their loss is from 400 to 600.

February 7. Rev. R. J. Stewart, of St. Paul's Church, Alexandria, Va., was arrested by Federal soldiers while holding services in his church, charged with being a secessionist, and for omitting to mention the name of the President of the United States in his prayer. He refused to leave the church and was dragged by force from the pulpit.

February 10. Newspaper office of the "Local News" was destroyed by Federal soldiers in Alexandria, Va. Large numbers of the citizens of Alexandria are arrested on charge of conspiracy against the Federal government..... Battle at Cobb's Point, near Elizabeth City, North Carolina. The Federals from Roanoke Island attack the Confederate steamers at batteries. Commodore Lynch made a brave defence, but was forced to retreat. The Federals captured 7 Confederate steamers and some army stores, guns, &c. Confederate loss 6 killed, 3 wounded. Federal loss 11 killed, 4 wounded.

February 11. Elizabeth City, North Carolina, partly burned by its inhabitants to prevent its falling into the enemy's hands.

February 12. Edenton and Hartford, North Carolina, occupied by the Federals.

February 12. Battle of the trenches. ⎫ Battle of Fort Donel-
February 13. Battle with gun boats. ⎬ son, Cumberland river,
February 15. Battle at Dover. ⎭ Tennessee

The fighting at Fort Donelson was the most bloody and desperate ever witnessed on the American continent, excepting, perhaps, the earlier conquest of Mexico by the Spaniards. The fighting commenced on Wednesday, 12th, the enemy was driven back with heavy loss; the battle of the 13th was fought mainly with the Federal gun boats. Seven boats attacked the Fort. The gun boats were entirely defeated by the heavy guns at the Fort. Some of the balls passed through a thickness of 25 inches of the iron and wood casing of the boats; 42 Federals were killed and wounded on the boats. The main fight was on Saturday, when our forces marched out of our entrenchments and attacked the enemy, killing not less than 1000, capturing 7 pieces of artillery, 250 prisoners and a large lot of small arms, blankets and knapsacks. The enemy had, with a large force, surrounded us, preparatory to cutting off our communication with Clarksville and Nashville. This was the cause of our going out and attacking them on Saturday. The result of the fight on Saturday made us feel triumphant. About sun down on Saturday we sent off the sick, wounded and prisoners in the two small boats we had at Donelson. Early in the night, our scouts brought up the information that fourteen steamboats were landing fresh troops one mile and a half below us. Three hours after our cavalry informed us that the enemy, in large force, had again surrounded us, occupying the position from which we had driven them in the morning.

The complete state of exhaustion of our army, and its manifest inability to make or sustain another attack, determined the surrender. The snow was six inches deep, the weather severely cold, and our men had been working and fighting for several days and nights, with no means of rest except when they found in the trenchments. They had been hurriedly carried there, without their tents or camp equippage.

Gens. Pillow and Floyd gave up their command to General Buckner, and ignominously left the Fort. The noble General Buckner refused to desert his men and was captured prisoner. As an evidence of the desperate character of the contest, the following paragraph is copied from a Federal account of the battle.

" The heaviest loss to any one of the Federal regiments at Fort Donelson, was the 11th Illinois, which went into the fight with 590 men and officers, and came out with 170. Two companies of this regiment, company K, Capt. Carter, of LaSalle. went into action with 62 men, and came out with nine! Company H, Capt. Contes, of Peru, went in with 51 men and came out with 10. This will give an idea of the hard fighting and terrible loss sustained."

The Federal loss is estimated at 1,200 killed, 2,000 wounded and 270 captured prisoners. Confederate loss 231 killed, 1,007 wounded, and 5,079 taken prisoners.

The whole amount of the Confederate force on first day of battle was nearly 13,829 men. The Federal force on the last day amounted to nearly 55,000 men.

February 14. Skirmish near New.Concord, Ky. Five Federals killed, several wounded.

February 15. Bowling Green, Ky., evacuated by Gen. Johnson and Confederate forces.

February 16. Tennessee Rolling Mills burned by the Federals. ....Skirmish near Moorfield, Va. Col. Ashby made a successful attack on a large force of Federals, killing many and driving them from their position.

February 17. Skirmish near Galveston, Texas. A large force of Federals, in attempting to make a landing near Galveston Bay, were surprised by the Confederates and driven back ; several Federals wounded.

Gen. Johnson notifies Gov. Harris that he cannot hold the city of Nashville against the Federals. Gov. Harris causes the State Archives to be removed to Memphis. The Governor and members of the Legislature leave Nashville for Memphis.

February 17-18-19. Great panic in Nashville, Tenn., caused by the fall of Fort Donelson and the threatened occupation of the city by the Federals. Great amount of army stores and provisions ($500,000 worth) destroyed, to prevent its falling into the enemy's hands. All the bridges and fortifications destroyed. Great numbers of people leave the city.

February 20. Winton, N. C., captured by the Federals. Confederate loss, 7 killed and 5 wounded.

February 22. Jefferson Davis inaugurated President of the Confederate States for the first regular term of six years.

February 24. Mayor Cheatham formally surrenders the city of Nashville to the Federals.

February 25. Skirmish near Occuquan, Va. Several Yankees reported killed.

February 26. The Federal forces, 40,000 strong, under Gen. Buell, occupy Nashville, Tenn.

February 22. Gen. Johnson falls back to Stephenson and Decator, on the line of the Memphis and Charleston Railroad.

March 1-2-3. Skirmish on the Tennessee River, near Savannah, between a party of Louisianians and Federal gun boats. The Federals defeated, 22 killed, 45 wounded. Confederate loss, 7 killed. 14 wounded.

Invasion of the Virginia Valley. Martinsburg and Charleston occupied by the Federals, under Gen. Banks.

Skirmishing near New Madrid, Mo., between the advancing Federals and Jeff. Thompson's forces; 20 Federals reported killed and 10 captured.

Columbus, Ky., evacuated by the Confederate forces. All the Confederate property removed to New Madrid and Island No. 10.

City of Pensacola and the Confederate Forts partly evacuated by the Confederates.

Gen. Bragg leaves Mobile for Memphis, Tenn. Fort Pickens partly evacuated by the Federals.

Brunswick, Geo., and Fernandina captured by the Federals. Commodore Dupont takes possession of all Confederate property. No resistance offered by the Confederates.

Columbus, Ky., occupied by the Federals, under General Cullum.

Martial law declared in Richmond, Va. John M. Botts and

several prominent Union men arrested in Richmond for aiding the enemy.

March 5. Martial law declared in Memphis, Tenn.

General Beauregard takes command of the army of the Mississippi. Headquarters at Jackson, Tenn.

March 5-6. Skirmish near New Creek, Western Virginia. Col. Ashby made a successful attack on a large force of Federals, routing them and capturing 40 prisoners. Confederate loss, 3 killed.

March 21. Battle of Valverde, Arizona Territory. The battle was fiercely contested, and undoubtedly the severest of the present war—as desperate as any on record for the amount of men engaged. The Confederate forces were mostly native Texans, who fought with all their well known courage and bravery, capturing the enemies batteries of 7 guns, at the point of the bayonet and knife, winning a glorious victory over the Federals. Maj. Lockridge, of the Confederates, was killed while leading a charge. Confederate loss, 86 killed and 156 wounded. Federal loss, 230 killed, 200 wounded and 500 captured prisoners. The Confederate force amounted to only 2,300; the Federals were 6,000 strong.

Running the blockade. Over 120 vessels have run the blockade from Southern ports since March, 1861, to the present time. During the past year 7 vessels have been captured by the Federals in attempting to run the blockade. It is estimated that 70 vessels have entered Southern ports during the same time.

The great debt and cost of the war to the Northern government:

"By a late statement of the chairman of the committee of Ways and Means in the Federal House of Representatives, it was shown that there will be required, in order to pay the outstanding debts of the treasury, for which there are no funds on hand, and to carry on the war until the next session of Congress, upwards of seven hundred millions of dollars. The aggregate debt, on the 1st day of December next, will be, by the same statement, $925,000.000. But Congress must also provide for the remainder of that current fiscal year, which will terminate on the 30th of June, 1862. Including these sums, the official Federal estimate is, that the public debt will amount on the 1st of July, 1863 —only sixteen months hence—to $1,350,000,000.

This estimate does not take into account the effects of a depreciated currency upon the cost to Government of its loans in bonds and treasury notes. Many additional millions must therefore be added to the aggregate to represent correctly the debt which will have to be redeemed, at some time, unless bankruptcy and repudiation come in first, with only a reasonable allowance for that excess of expenditure over estimates, which is universal at Washington ; the Federal debt will, by the middle of next year, reach fully up to fifteen hundred millions of dollars."

March 7. McClellan commences moving his troops from Washington to the Peninsula, Va.

March 6-7-8. Battle of Elkhorn, or Pea Ridge, Ark. A great and desperate battle was fought between the Federals, under Generals Curtis and Seigel, with a force of 20,000 men, and the Confederates, under Generals Price, McCulloch and VanDorn, with 14,000 men. After three days hard fighting the Confederates withdrew on account of the death of McCulloch. Confederate loss, 169 killed, 431 wounded and 200 taken prisoners. Federal loss, 390 killed, 900 wounded and 300 captured prisoners· [From Gen. VanDorn's official report.] Generals McCulloch and McIntosh, of the Confederates were killed. Gen. Seigel of the Federals, badly wounded. Thirty Federals were scalped by the Confederate Indians in the battle.

March 7. Leesburg evacuated by the Confederates; large amounts of Confederate and private property destroyed to prevent its falling into the enemy's hand.

March 8-9. Naval battle in Hampton Roads, near Norfolk, Va. The new Confederate steamer Virginia, (late Merrimac) otherwise known as the "Norfolk Turtle," "Colossus of the Roads," attacks five of the largest Federal blockading ships. The Virginia was assisted in the attack by the Confederate gun boats, "Patrick Henry," "Jamestown," "Yorktown" and "Teaser." The Virginia won a most glorious victory, having destroyed the following war vessels : Congress, burnt, 430 men, 50 guns ; Cumberland, sunk, 360 men, 22 guns ; Minnessota, riddled, 550 men, 40 guns; St. Lawrence, peppered, 480 men, 50 guns ; gun boats two or three disabled, 120 men, 6 guns ; Forts silenced, 200 men, 20 guns ; Ericsson, 150 men, 3 guns. Total—men, 2890—guns, 230. The Virginia also engaged the Federal iron clad vessel "Monitor." The encounter was a drawn battle, both vessels retiring at the same time. The Monitor was considerably damaged. The Virginia suffered only a trifling loss on the breaking of her iron prow. Federal loss estimated at 700 killed, wounded and drowned. Confederate loss, 9 killed, 18 wounded.

The self abnegating heroism of Capt. Buchanan, commander of the Virginia in the recent memorable conflict, will be generally appreciated when it is known that his younger and favorite brother was the purser of the frigate Congress, at which the fire of the Virginia was most pertinaciously directed, and is supposed to have perished on board of her.

March 1. Skirmishing near Charleston, Va., the federals routed and several killed, and 17 taken prisoners.

March 7-8-9. The Confederate forces evacuates Centreville, Manassas and Occuquan, and falls back to a new line of defence on the Rappahannock River, Va. In retiring from Manassas, everything that could give aid and comfort to the enemy was destroyed ; guns, ammunition and stores were brought off in good order; and the railroad tracks, both that leading to Manassas Gap and that to Orange, torn up. The continuation of the former to Mount Jackson, in the direction of Stanton, will also be torn up as fast as General Jackson, of the Army of the Shenandoah, retires to the mountains. The New York Post says the retreat from Manassas was the most masterly effort in ancient or modern warfare. That it changes the character of the war, and protracts the contest for a long time.

March 8. Traffic in gold and silver. Gold and silver was sold by speculators as high as 80 per cent. premium in New Orleans, and in Memphis, Tennessee, gold was reported to have been sold at 140 per cent. premium. Dealing in gold and silver was suppressed by authority in New Orleans.

March 8-9. Capturing and harrassing the enemy near Nashville, Tenn. The gallant "partizan leader," Captain Morgan, is making himself famous in exploits; he is giving the enemy great trouble. During a late skirmish, there were sixty Federals captured, also a large amount of property belonging to the enemy.

March 9. Skirmish near Nashville, Tenn. Captain Scott made an attack on the Federals, completely routing them; killing thirty and capturing a large amount of guns, ammunition, &c. Confederate loss, 3 killed, 5 wounded.

March 11. The Federal army occupies Manassas, Va. On Tuesday evening, being about to be attacked by 18,000 of the enemy, General Jackson, with his small force of only 5000 fell back from Winchester, and stayed that night about four miles from that town. On Wednesday morning 1000 of the enemy took possession of Winchester. On the afternoon of Wednesday, Gen. Shields' column advanced toward Newtown, but were met and driven into Winchester by Col. Ashby's command. Before evacuating Winchester, General Jackson succeeded in removing all his stores, baggage, etc., so that not a dollar's worth of public property fell into the hands of the enemy. Skirmish near Cumberland Gap, Tenn. The Federals were severely repulsed and forty taken prisoners. Confederate loss, 2 killed and 1 wounded.

March 12. The dark days of the Confederacy. The peaceably defensive policy of the Confederate Government, during the past six months, has nerved the Federal Government to redoubled exertions in the scheme of conquering the South. The consequence to the Confederacy has been the loss of several important battles, reverses and loss of positions, not a few of which has been owing to bad Generalship on the part of Confederate commanders. The timid and discontented portion of the Southern people see in such reverses the doom of the South. But all true Southerners feel confident that the worst has come, and are certain of glorious success in the future. A new spirit of energy has been infused into the government, and the army, all true patriots, are resolved to conquer or die for the cause of freedom and their rights.... Jacksonville, Florida, occupied by the Federals, who erect batteries. The people destroyed part of the city before surrendering to the Federals.... Skirmish near Paris, Tenn. The Confederates withdrew their pickets.

March 12–13. Skirmishing at Eastport, Tenn. The Confederate batteries attacked by the Federal gunboats: no damage done.... Attack on New Madrid, Mo. The Federals advanced and attacked the Confederates at New Madrid, a brisk fight took place, during which the Federals were repulsed and driven back; during the following night the Confederates suddenly evacuated the place, as it was expected that the Federals were returning with large reinforcements to renew the attack. The Confederates left behind a large number of cannon, guns and army stores. Confederate loss during the fight 16 killed, 9 wounded. Federal loss 25 killed, 47 wounded.

March 13. Hon. W. L. Yancey, Confederate minister, arrives in New Orleans from Europe, he makes a speech to the citizens of New Orleans, during which he said that "He came back convinced that we had no friends in Europe, that we must fight the battle alone, and rely only on our own firm hearts."....The Federals landed a force of 2,500 men, and attacks and capture the Confederate batteries at Newbern, N. C. The Confederates, who numbered only 700, fought bravely before surrendering. After capturing the batteries the Federals advanced to the city of Newbern and shelled the place, before the women and children could escape. Confederate loss, 45 killed, 55 wounded and 202 taken prisoners. Federal loss estimated at 650 killed and wounded.... General Lee assigned the command of the Confederate army under the consent of President Davis.... Andy Johnson, the traitor, arrives in Nashville, Tennessee, and assumes the office of Governor under Federal authority. Johnson was accompanied by his fellow traitors Etheridge and Maynard.

March 14. General Fremont appointed to a new command in the West—"The Mountain Department."....A party of Confederate cavalry was surprised by the enemy near Cumberland Gap, Tennessee. Five Confederates killed and wounded.

March 15. Bombardment of New Madrid and Island No. 10 commences.... The Federal Senate has passed the bill for the "occupation and cultivation" of such cotton lands as the Federal armies may acquire in the South.... They are going to take the cotton lands, and work negroes thereon for the benefit of the government. It is, to be sure, an absurd project and will be, whenever attempted, a miserable and costly failure. It is a Yankee scheme, to become slaveholders in fact, while giving the slaves a nominal freedom; to work them by agents, underlings and drivers, without one motive to produce that kindly humanity, which is the glory of the system in Southern hands. It is a grand national sham, which has in it all the elements of cruelty to the negro, and the certainty of breaking up speedily under circumstances of wretchedness to the poor slave, and losses to the speculating government.... Cavalry fight near Warrenton, Va. Gen. Stewart engaged a large force of Federal cavalry and succeeded in completely routing them, killing forty and captured one hundred with their horses, &c. Confederate loss was six killed and one hundred and eighty wounded.... General McClellan, commander of the Federal army, takes the field in person, commanding the "army of the Potomac" he delivers a long speech to his soldiers.

March 17. Attack and bombardment at Island 10, Mississippi river, continued by the Federals. The Island is vigorously defended.

March 18. Skirmish near Point Pleasant, Mo. The Federals erecting batteries below Island 10. The Confederate gunboats advances and shells the batteries, a brisk firing took place when the Federals retired from their batteries. Three of the Confederate steamers were slightly damaged. A gun bursted on board one of the boats while being fired. No lives lost.

March 19. Financial condition of the Confederate States. We learn that the official report of the Secretary of the Treasury shows that our financial system has proved adequate to supplying all the wants of the Government, notwithstanding the unexpected and very large increase of expenditures resulting from the great augmentation in the necessary means of defence. The report exhibits the gratifying fact that we have no floating debt; that the credit of the Government is unimpaired, and that the total expenditure of the Government for the year has been, in round numbers, one hundred and seventy millions of dollars—less than one third of the sum wasted by the enemy in his vain effort to conquer us—less than the value of a single article of export—the cotton crop of the year.

March 22. Fighting at Cumberland Gap, Tennessee. The Federals were repulsed with considerable loss. Confederate loss 2 killed, 5 wounded....Andy Johnson, the Yankee military Governor of Tennessee, makes a speech at Nashville in which he adroitly seeks to throw all the blame for the present condition of affairs upon the South....In his opinion, Lincoln is our friend, and has no idea of interfering with our institutions.

March 22. A federal gunboat with a large force on board attempted to land and occupy a fortification on Mosquito Inlet, Florida. The Federals were fired on by a party of Confederates and forced to retreat. Federal loss 9 killed, 15 wounded and 2 captured.

March 23. Battle at Bolton's Mill, or Kernstown, Va., Gen. (Stone Wall) Jackson with 6000 men engaged the Federals under General Shields, numbering 18,000 strong, after a severe contest the Federals were repulsed and fell back. General Jackson also fell back for reinforcements. Federal loss 175 killed, 460 wounded. Confederate loss 93 killed, 163 wounded and 230 captured.... Guerrilla fighting near Jefferson City, Mo. Federal cavalry attacked Guerrilla parties dispersing them, 78 were captured prisoners, 3 killed, the Federals lost during the attack 400 killed and wounded.

March 25. The Federal bombardment at Island No. 10 has been continued for nine days, without doing any material damage to the fortifications. Two Federal gunboats were sunk and three badly disabled during the attack. It is estimated that the enemy fired 2500 shot and shell at the batteries on island 10 and vicinity during the first four days of the bombardment, and wasted 60,000 pounds of powder, with iron in proportion, killing one and wounding two of our men. The shells which they throw at us, weigh from 190 to 200 pounds. It is estimated that one thousand Federals were killed and wounded during the bombardment....Bay

St. Louis. A lively naval battle occurred in this vicinity to-day between the Confederate gunboats Oregon and Pamlico and the famous Federal gunboat New London. The fight lasted three hours, and resulted in the defeat of the New London.... Peppering the Yankees, St. Mary's river, Georgia. A Federal gunboat with a large force on board went in pursuit of a Confederate steamer. The Federals unexpectedly encountered a body of Confederates who opened fire on them, killing forty and wounding sixteen Yankees. The Confederates retired without loss.

March 27. Battle of Glorietta, New Mexico. The Federals completely routed, with a loss of 700 killed and captured. Confederate loss, 68 killed and wounded.

March 29. Another attack on the Yankees at Edisto, North Carolina. General Evans, with one thousand men, proceeded to attack the enemy, which was supposed to be 2500, but found them to be 5000 to 6000. The Confederates drove in the enemy's pickets, killing one, mortally wounded and capturing twenty. We retired in good order.... Fight in Polk county, Mo. An engagement took place between the Confederate forces and State troops; large number of Federals killed and wounded. Confederate loss reported to be 15 killed and wounded.... THE PECULIARITIES OF THE DAY.—In the whirl of passing events we scarcely notice the strange things that are daily happening and existing around us. How astonishing it will appear, in a few years, that a time existed when planters raised corn and potatoes, fattened hogs and cultivated garden vegetables, while cotton was by universal consent neglected, and this at a time when cotton was worth in Liverpool 28 cents a pound, yet selling on the plantation at 5 cents.... Our newspapers have felt the martial influence as strongly as other things. They never had so much variety as now, since Faust first pulled the press; they are of all sizes and colors, and sometimes contain four pages, and sometimes two. They are short enough for a pocket handkerchief one day, and big enough for a table cloth another. They assume as many hues as Niagara in the sunshine, and are by turns blue, yellow, green, red, purple, grey and common brown packing paper.... How odd it will be to remember that certain merchandize was forbidden to be brought into the city, and certain kinds of produce to be taken out; and that in many places in the markets and stores, dealers could sell only at prices dictated to them by a provost marshal. .... Politics are dead. A political enemy is a curiosity only read of in books. We have no whigs, no democrats, no know nothings, no nothing. Our amusements have revolutionized. The winter has passed by without a company having been engaged at the theatre, or a single circus having spread tent. Our people have done their own playing and their own singing, and the ladies have spent the mornings in sewing coarse shirts or pantaloons for the soldier to wear, and sung in public at night to gain money for the soldiers' equipments.... The President's message to Congress, asking the repeal of all existing military laws and making conscript laws instead, recommends a law subjecting every man between 18 and 35 years to militia service.... Skirmish near Rappahanock River, Va. Colonel Wheat engaged the enemy, driving them back, killing 3, and capturing 29 Yankees.

March 30. Federal raid at Union city, Tenn. A large force of Federals surprised a small squad of Confederates at Union city, after a sharp engagement the Federals retreated; Confederate loss 2 killed, 7 wounded and thirty taken prisoners. The enemy captured a large number of horses and army stores; 2 Federals killed.

March 31. Three companies of Georgians attacked the Yankees on Wilmington Island, killing one and wounding several; Georgians lost one killed.... Skirmish near Jacksonville, Fla. A detachment of Colonel Dilworth's Guard attacked the Federals, killing 4 and capturing 3 of the enemy; Confederate loss 2 killed and wounded.

April 1. A party of Federals secretly landed at Island 10, and spiked several guns of the Confederate battery, and successfully escaped from the Island.

April 4. Several Federal gunboats and transports passed Island 10 during a heavy storm and under cover of the night.... Naval engagement near Bay St. Louis, Miss. The Confederate gunboats engaged the Federal boats. The Federals withdrew, one of their boats being badly damaged; Confederate loss 1 wounded.

April 5. Two thousand Federals landed at Pass Christian, Mississippi, and attacked the Confederate camps. The Confederates being in small force, were compelled to retire, no one hurt. The Federals after committing many depredations on private property, returned to their boats.

April 5–6. Skirmishing near Yorktown, Va. The Federals are reported to be landing in large force in the neighborhood. A heavy battle will take place at an early day.

April 6. Skirmish in East Tennessee. Colonel Vaughn has penetrated Scott county, Tennessee, to Huntsville, whipped the enemy and routed him, and brought off meat, shoes, cattle and horses. He killed about forty of the enemy, and took seventeen

prisoners, losing only five men. He also destroyed all the commissary stores he could not bring away.
April 6-7. Battle of Shiloh, Tenn. The Confederates, under Gens. Beauregard and Johnson, advanced from their encampment and attacked the enemy. The battle commenced early on Sunday morning. The fighting was the most terrible of any during the war, both sides contending with great desperation. Towards evening the Federals commenced falling back and retreated to their gunboats on the Tennessee river, being severely defeated, leaving behind nearly all their batteries (18) which were taken by the Confederates. General Prentiss, with 3000 men, were taken prisoners. An immense number of guns, army stores, &c., were captured by the Confederates. The lamented General Albert S. Johnson was killed early in the evening. During the night of Sunday, the Federals were largely reinforced by General Buell with 25,000 troops, and on Monday morning the battle was renewed with vigor, and continued throughout the day. The Federals were again repulsed and defeated, retiring to their gunboats. The Confederates moved back to their positions after accomplishing a most brilliant success.... The Confederate forces in the two days' fight numbered 38,000 men. The Federal force on the first day's fight was over 58,000, on the second day the Federals were reinforced to 70,000 men. The Confederate loss was 1,728 killed, 8,012 wounded, and 959 missing; Federal loss, 2,500 killed and 9,800 wounded and 3,700 taken prisoners. The Federals suffered severely in the loss of officers, nearly all being killed, wounded and captured. Generals Sherman, Tom Crittenden, Major Wallace and Lew Wallace were killed. Generals Grant, Smith and Buell were wounded.
April 7. The loss of Island 10, Mississipppi river. After being bravely defended from a constant bombardment of twenty days, the Federal gunboats, with a large force, succeeded in passing below the island and attacked the rear batteries, and compelled the Confederates to leave their guns and surrender the island. The Confederates, before surrendering, destroyed nearly all the property on the island, spiking their guns. The steamboats, floating batteries and wharf boats were scuttled and sunk. About one thousand of the Confederates escaped from the island, after suffering severe hardships. General Mackall and three thousand men were taken prisoners on the island. Many of the Confederates were drowned in making their escape through the overflowed swamps near the island.... Picket skirmish at Shepardstown, North Carolina. The Confederates killed two Yankees and cap-

tured nine... Reported insurrection in Southern Illinois. A general disposition on the part of the people to resist the payment of the war tax, followed by a protest of some twenty members of the Legislature, against the doctrines of Lincoln's message, is said to be the origin of the difficulty. The recusant members were arrested by the abolition authorities. Trouble followed, which a single regiment found it impossible to quell, when several others were sent out and the peace party was crushed at the point of the bayonet.

April 8. When our army commenced retiring from Shiloh on Monday evening, General Breckinridge's brigade, with the cavalry, was ordered to bring up the rear, and prevent the enemy from cutting off any of our trains. The cavalry mentioned were attacked by a Federal force of two regiments of infantry and one of cavalry, the latter being in the advance. At the first fire the cavalry of the enemy turned and fled, actually breaking the ranks of their own infantry in endeavoring to escape the missiles of the Confederates. The result of this dashing affair was—Federal loss, killed and wounded, two hundred and fifty, and forty-eight prisoners; Confederates, ten killed and wounded.

April 11. Battle of Fort Pulaski, Georgia. The fort was attacked by a large force of Federals. After a most gallant defence the Confederates surrendered. Three balls had entered the magazine, and a clear breach had been made in it. The balls were conical, steel pointed, and propelled with such force as to pass entirely through the wall at nearly every fire. No lives were lost during the bombardment, and only four were wounded..,.. The Federals take possession of Huntsville, Alabama, and Decatur, on the Memphis and Charleston Railroad; the enemy seized several railroad cars at Decatur.

April 13. Engagement at Fort Jackson and Fort Philippe, La. (The first firing since the forts were built.) Several Federal gunboats commenced bombarding Fort Jackson at "long range." The Fort promptly replied by opening their batteries.

April 12–13. Heavy skirmishing continues daily on the Peninsula, Va. The Federals repulsed in every attack. In the fight on the 12th the Confederates lost 5 kilied and 13 wounded; the Federal loss was much heavier.... The seige of Fort Macon, North Carolina, commences. The Federals land a large force near the fort. Col. White, who commanded the Confederates, sent out a detachment and gave them battle, repulsing the Federals after a hot contest. Confederate loss, 15 killed and several wounded.

April 16. Skirmish near White Marsh Island, Georgia. The Federals repulsed with a loss of 20 killed and wounded. Confederate loss, 5 killed and 4 wounded.... Battle of Lee's Farm, Va. The Federals made a spirited attack on the Confederate lines. After a hard contested battle the Federals were severely defeated. Confederate loss, 30 killed and 55 wounded. Federal loss, 385 killed and wounded. The Confederates were commanded by Gen. Magruder.... Skirmishing near Fredericksburg, Va. The Confederates were attacked and driven into the city with severe loss. The Federals under Gen. McDowell advances and compels the Confederates to evacuate the city ; large amounts of public and private property was destroyed during the hasty evacuation.

April 18. Bombardment of Forts Jackson and St. Phillippe, below New Orleans, continued.

April 19. Battle of South Mills, or "Sawyers Lane," Va. The Federals were defeated. Confederate loss, 18 killed and 50 wounded. Federal loss, 200 killed and wounded.... Fight near Elizabeth City, North Carolina. The Confederates were defeated with a loss of 6 killed and 31 wounded.... The Confederate Senate passed a bill providing for the organization of partizan bands.... Skirmishing continues on the Peninsula, Va. The Confederates generally repelling all attacks of the enemy ; in the battle to-day, the Confederate loss was 18 killed and 50 wounded; the Federal loss was very heavy.

April 20. The seige of Fort Jackson, La., continues day and night. Such a tremendous bombardment has never been known in modern war. It is estimated that the enemy have fired 370,000 pounds of powder, and 1000 tons of iron. No damage has yet been done to the fort. Two gunboats have been sunk and one disabled.

April 23. Guerrilla fighting in Logan county, Va. A large party of Federals were routed, with a loss of 50 killed and wounded.

April 24. Great gunboat battle above Fort Jackson. On the morning of 24th inst., the Federal fleet succeeded in passing the forts. The fleet was immediately attacked by the Confederate gunboats, when a most desperate battle took place. The Confederate boats were all disabled and sunk. The Federal fleet advanced up the river to New Orleans. The Confederate fleet consisted of 10 gunboats, including the great ram Louisiana and "Manassas." The Federal fleet consisted of 8 mortar boats and 14 war steamers, including 4 iron clads. The Federals lost 3 war vessels ; one of the largest vessels, the Pensacola, with a crew of 400 persons, was sunk with all on board. Confederate loss, on board of the boats, 38 killed and 125 wounded. Federal loss estimated at 1000 killed, wounded and missing. The garrison, under Gen. Duncan, still held possession of the forts.

April 25. The Federal fleet attacks the Chalmette Batteries, below New Orleans; after a fight of two hours, the batteries were silenced.... On the night of the 25th inst., the Confederate garrison at Fort Jackson mutinously revolted, spiking their guns, which compelled the brave Gen. Duncan to surrender the forts to the Federals. The bombardment of the fort lasted seven days, unintermittingly. Sixteen lives were lost inside the fort, and 26 wounded. No injury was done to the guns; the fort could have been held, had the garrison continued faithful.... Fort Macon, North Carolina, surrenders conditionally after a well contested defence. Confederate loss inside the fort, was 7 killed and 18 wounded.

April 25–27. Skirmishing in Tennessee and North Alabama between Colonel Scott's cavalry and the Federals under General Mitchell. Colonel Scott captures a large amount of stores and takes several prisoners.

April 26. Great excitement in New Orleans. The advance fleet of Federal gunboats arrives in front of New Orleans, a party of Federals landed and demanded the surrender of the city; immense quantities of sugar and molasses was destroyed to prevent its falling into the Federal hands; General Lovell retreats with his troops up the Jackson railroad.

April 27–28. Battle of Cassville, Mo. Confederates defeated with a loss of 30 killed and wounded, and 62 taken prisoners.

April 28. Skirmish at Pittsburg Landing, Tenn.; Federal loss 27 killed, wounded and prisoners.

April 28–29. Heavy skirmishing at Cumberland Gap, Tenn.; Federals repulsed with a loss of 100 killed, and 284 wounded; Confederate loss 27 killed and 61 wounded.

April 29. Fight at Bridgeport, Tenn.; Confederates defeated.

April 30, and May 1. Forts Macomb and Pike, on Lake Pontchatrain, La., was destroyed and abandoned by the Confederates; four Confederate gunboats were destroyed in a very hasty manner.

May 1. The city of New Orleans formally occupied by the Yankee General Butler.... General Morgan captures a large amount of Federal stores at Pulaski, Tenn.

May 5. Skirmish near Lebanon, Tenn.; the Confederates

were severely defeated, and lost 20 killed and 35 wounded and 45 captured prisoners.... Battle of Williamsburg, Va.; a signal victory was gained by the Confederates, under General Johnson, over the Federals, under General McClellan ; Confederate loss, 520 killed and 1100 wounded; Federal loss, 1000 killed and 2700 wounded.

May 7. Battle of Barhamsville, or West Point, Va.; the Yankees were badly defeated.

May 8. Battle at McDowel's, or Sitlington's Mill, Va.; Gen. Stonewall Jackson achieved a great victory over the Federals, who were commanded by General Milroy ; Confederate loss, 350 killed and wounded; Federal loss, 175 killed and 255 wounded.

May 9. The Confederate forces evacuates Pensacola navy yard, destroying vast amounts of property.... Battle of Farmington, (near Corinth,) Tenn.; the Federals, under General Pope, were badly defeated and put to route, with a loss of 35 killed and 100 wounded ; Confederate loss, 15 killed and 109 wounded.

May 10. Skirmish near Elkhorn River, North Carolina; Confederate loss, 5 killed, 7 wounded ; Federal loss, 7 killed and 45 wounded.

May 11. Colonel Morgan captures a train of cars on the Louisville railroad, near Cave City.

May 10–11. Fighting at Parisburg, or Gibbs Courthouse, Va. The Federals were defeated and driven from the town, with a loss of 120 killed and wounded, and 100 captured ; large quantities of Federal stores were taken ; Confederate loss, 1 killed and 14 wounded.

May 11. Skirmish near Pollocksville, North Carolina; the Federals defeated with a loss of 10 killed; Confederate loss, 3 wounded and 4 captured.

May 12. The advance fleet of Federal gunboats arrives at Natchez, Miss., and demands the surrender of the city.

May 13. Skirmishing near Purdy, Tenn.; several killed on both sides.

May 15. The fleet of Federal gunboats attacks the half finished batteries at Drewry's Bluff, Va ; the Federals were repulsed with a loss of 13 killed and 11 wounded; Confederate loss, 7 killed and 8 wounded.

May 17. Battle of Princeton, Va.; the Confederates, under General Heth, defeated the Yankees ; Confederate loss, 5 killed and 17 wounded ; Federal loss, 150 killed and wounded.

May 18. Skirmish near City Point, Va.; Federals repulsed, with a loss of 8 killed and 9 captured.

May 18-19-20. Skirmishing near Corinth, Miss.; several severe fights occurred without important results; the Federals generally worsted; in the action of the 20th inst. 25 Confederates were killed and 65 wounded.

May 18. . The advance division of Farragut's Federal fleet arrives below Vicksburg, Miss.; the surrender of the city was demanded.

May 19. Skirmish near Warrenton, Va.; result was 4 Yankees killed; 2 Confederates killed.... Skirmish below Vicksburg, Miss.; 4 Yankees killed and wounded.

May 18-19. Battle near Searcy, Arkansas; Federals defeated; Confederate loss 5 killed and 11 wounded; Federal loss 45 killed and wounded.

May 21. Bombardment of Fort Pillow, Tenn., resumed....; The Federals commenced bombarding the batteries at Cole's Island, near Savannah.

May 20. A party of Federals in approaching St. Marks, Fla., were surprised by the Confederates; 17 Yankees were killed.

May 23-24. Battle at Front Royal, Va.; the Federals were defeated and driven from the town; 1470 were taken prisoners; large quantities of Federal stores were captured.

May 23-24. Battle of Lewisburg, Western Va.; the Confederates were defeated after a hard fight; Confederate loss, 230 killed and wounded; Federal loss was much heavier.

May 24. The Federal army, under Gen. Banks, in retreat from Front Royal, is pursued by the Confederates, who captures several prisoners, and takes large quantities of stores, &c., near Middleton, Va.... Skirmish on the New Kent Road, Tenn.; the Yankees repulsed; Confederate loss 2 killed and 5 wounded.

May 23-24. Skirmishing at Garnett's Farm, near Richmond, Va. A severe engagement took place, in which the Confederates were defeated, with a loss of 100 killed and wounded; Federal loss, 122 killed and wounded.

May 25. Battle at Winchester, Va. General Stonewall Jackson defeats the Federal army, and takes 800 prisoners, and captures vast quantities of Federal stores; Confederate loss, 124 killed and wounded; Federal loss, 50 killed and 259 wounded.

May 26. Skirmish near Grand Gulf, Miss.; Federals repulsed ....The first bombarding at Vicksburg, Miss., takes place.

May 26-27. Skirmish at Hanover Courthouse, Va.. A desperate engagement took place, in which the Federals were defeated with a loss of 63 killed and 279 wounded; Confederate loss 90 killed and 232 wounded.

May 28. A Confederate scouting party was surprised near Oakfield, Fla., and one man killed.
May 28-29. Corinth, Miss., evacuated by the Confederates, under General Beauregard; skirmishing occurred during the retreat; General Price engaged the Yankees and repulsed them.
May 31. General Stonewall Jackson falls back from Winchester, Va.
May 31, and June 1. Battle of Seven Pines, or Fair Oaks, Va. The Federal army, under General McClellan, was defeated by the Confederates under Gens Hill, Longstreet, and Huger; Federal loss, 2070 killed, and 4900 wounded, and 550 prisoners; Confederate loss, 1035 killed, and 2700 wounded.
June 1. Fight near Stransburg, Va. Gen. Jackson defeats the Federals under Fremont.
June 2-5. Skirmishing near Washington, N. C. The Federals defeated, with a loss of 9 killed and 17 wounded; Confederate loss, 3 killed and 4 wounded; Colonel Singletary was killed.
June 3. Skirmish on James Island, near Savannah.; the Federals repulsed, 20 captured prisoners; Confederate loss, 2 killed and 8 wounded.
June 4. Fort Pillow evacuated by the Confederate forces.... Fight near Sweeden's Cave, Tenn· A party of Confederates were surrounded by a large force of Federals; the Confederates cut their way out with a loss of 15 killed.
June 5. Skirmishing on the Chickahominy, Va. Four Confederates wounded....Skirmish near Harrisburg, Virginia. The Federals repulsed; Confederate loss 40 killed and 100 wounded; General Turner Ashby killed.
June 6. Naval battle in front of Memphis, Tenn. The Yankee fleet, under Com. Davis, attacks our gunboats; after three hours hard fighting we were defeated ; our loss 80 killed and wounded, and 75 taken prisoners, and four gunboats sunk.... The city of Memphis formally surrendered and was occupied by the Yankees.
June 7. W. B. Mumford was publicly hung in the city of New Orleans, by the order of Gen. Butler, for tearing down the United States flag from the mint.
June 7-8. Fighting on James Island, near Savannah; the Yankees were again repulsed; our loss 55 killed and wounded.
June 8-9. Battle of Port Republic, Va. Gen. Jackson defeats the Yankees under Gen. Shields and Fremont; our loss 550 killed and wounded; Yankee loss 1000 killed and wounded, and 700 taken prisoners.

June 10. Skirmish near York River Railroad, Va. Yankees defeated with a loss of 45 killed; our loss 4 killed.

June 11. Battle of Cross Keys, Va. Gen. Ewell defeats the Federals under Fremont. Federal loss 1,000 killed and wounded; Confederate loss 124 killed and wounded.

June 14–15 Gen. Stuart makes a successful raid among the Yankees near Hanover Court House, and destroys a large amount of Federal property and captures 175 prisoners. The brave Capt. Latane was killed in the action.

June 14. Battle of Languelle, on White River, Ark. Federals defeated.

June 16. Battle of Secessionville S. C.. A complete victory was gained over the Federals. Confederate loss 40 killed and 100 wounded, 26 missing; Federal less 300 killed and wounded.

June 18. Skirmish near Richmond, Va. Federals repulsed; Confederate loss 9 wounded.

June 25. Battle on the Williamsburg Road, Va. The First Louisiana Regiment engaged Sickles' Brigade. After a sharp fight the Yankees were driven back. Confederate loss 200 killed and wounded.

Battles of the Chickahominy, before Richmond, Va. June 26, battle of Mechanicsville; 27, battle of Gainesville; 29, battle of Frazer's Farm; 30, battle of Willis' Church; July 1, battle of Malvern Hill. The great Federal army under Gen. McClellan was defeated and utterly routed after seven days hard fighting. Confederate loss 1,350 killed and 4,420 wounded; Federal loss 1,585 killed. 7,800 wounded and 6,000 taken prisoners.

June 28. Great bombardment at Vicksburg, Miss. Seven of the Federal gunboats advanced in front of the city, passing the batteries, when a most terrific bombardment took place. No injury was sustained by the forts.

July 1. A Confederate battery opened fire on the enemy near Coggins' Point, James River. After a sharp contest the Federals retreated. Confederate loss 2 killed and 6 wounded.

July 3. Gen. McClellan evacuates his position before Richmond, Va., and retires to the James River.

July 4. The army of the Potomac was originally 230,000 strong. Prior to the 5th of April, according to the testimony of the Assistant Secretary of War, McClellan had 120,000 men at Yorktown. From the time he landed at Yorktown to the beginning of the great battles, he lost, it seems, in various ways, 73,-000, and between the landing and close of the seven days' fighting, 98,000 out of 158,000 had been killed, had died in the swamps, or had by sickness been rendered unfit for service. In less than a year, he lost nearly 100,000 out of 230,000 men, without accomplishing anything.

July 8. Skirmish at Culpeper Cross Roads, Va. The Federals defeated.

July 13. Col. Forrest attacks and captures the Yankee garrison at Murfreesboro, Tenn. Federal loss 60 killed and 140 wounded and 1,900 taken prisoners.

July 15. Skirmish at Fayetteville, Ark. Confederates defeated..... The great ram Arkansas engages the Federal fleet near Vicksburg Miss., and successfully run the gauntlet between 30 gun and mortar boats, without sustaining any injury. Nearly all of the Federal fleet was damaged, and one sunk by the guns of the Arkansas. Federal loss on board the boats was 63 killed and 84 wounded; Confederate loss on board the Arkansas 9 killed and 4 wounded. The Arkansas came down and moored under the batteries at Vicksburg; about seven o'clock in the evening five of the Federal gunboats came down and attempted to cut the Arkansas from the shore; the effort was unsuccessful, and the fleet was driven off.

July 21. Skirmish near Carmel Church, Va. The Federals claimed a victory.

July 22. The Confederate and Federal Governments make an agreement for a general exchange of prisoners..... Lincoln publishes an order authorizing the confiscating of Confederate property for the use of Federal soldiers..... The Federal fleet makes another attack on the ram Arkansas, in front of Vicksburg. The fleet was repulsed..... The Confederates attack the Yankees at Florence, Ala., and destroy a large amount of stores.

July 23. Gen. Bragg leaves Tupelo, Miss., for Kentucky.

July 24. The combined Federal fleet retires and abandons the seige of Vicksburg, without accomplishing anything, after a seige of six weeks. No injury was sustained by any of the batteries at Vicksburg. The number of shells thrown into the city and at the batteries will amount to 25,000. The casualties in the city was one woman and one negro man killed, and among the soldiers on guard and at the batteries there was 22 killed and wounded. The lower bombarding fleet, under command of Coms. Farragut and Porter, consisted of 18 gun and mortar boats, 5 sloops of war and 70 transports; the upper fleet consisted of 11 gunboats and rams, and 13 transports, under command of Com. Davis. It is estimated that 500 Federals died from sickness during the seige of Vicksburg.

July 25. Col. Armstrong attacks the Yankees at Courtland, Ala., and captures 133 prisoners.....Col. Kelly attacks and routs a large party of Federals at Jonesboro, Tenn. Federal loss 9 killed and 5 wounded; 3 Confederates wounded.

July 26. Guerilla fighting in Missouri. The Confederate guerillas have been successful in several attacks on the Federals in Missouri.

July 29. Fight at Mt. Sterling, Ky. The Confederates were repulsed with a loss of 13 killed and 20 wounded; Federal loss 3 killed and 7 wounded.

July 31. Gen. Morgan's official report of his successful raids through Kentucky and Tennessee, amounts to the capturing of 20 towns, and taking of 1,200 prisoners, and destroying Federal property to the amount of $600,000. The Confederate loss in all the engagements was 23 killed and 47 wounded.....Engagement on the James River near Richmond, Va. The Federal fleet repulsed. Confederate loss 3 killed and 4 wounded.

July 27. Skirmishing near Bolivar, Tenn. The Confederates repulsed with a loss of 15 killed and wounded.

July 27–30. Skirmishing near Stevenson, Ala. The Yankees defeated in two severe fights. Loss of both sides, 17 killed and 40 wounded.

July 28. Battle of Moore's Mill, Mo. (near Fulton.) The Confederates were routed with a loss of 22 killed and 60 wounded.

July 28. Skirmishing near Humboldt, Tenn,

June —. The Confederates attacked and captured the Federal garrison at Summerville, Va. Federal loss, 6 killed and 23 wounded. Confederate loss, 5 wounded.

Aug. 1. Bombardment on James River, near Westover. Four Federals killed and 8 wounded.

Aug. 2. Fight near Madison, Ark. Gen. Parsons surprised a Federal camp and put the Yankees to flight.

Aug. 2. Cavalry skirmish at Orange Court House, Va. Confederates defeated, 2 killed and 10 wounded.

Aug. 3. Skirmish at Cox's Mill Creek, Va. Confederate loss 2 killed and 5 wounded.

Aug, 3. Fight near Memphis, Tenn. The Confederates under Jeff. Thompson defeated with a loss of three killed and five wounded.

August 4. Skirmish near Hanover Court House, Va. Gen. Stuart captures 30 Yankees. Federal stores destroyed.

August 5–6. Fighting near Malvern Hill, Va. The Federals

after a hard battle defeated the Confederates with a loss of five killed and nine wounded. The Federals afterwards evacuated the place. Federal loss 30 killed and wounded.

August 5. Battle of Tazewell, near Cumberland Gap, Tenn. Federals repulsed with a loss of 94 killed and wounded. Confederate loss 21 killed and 35 wounded'

August 5. Battle of Baton Rouge, La. The Confederates under Gen. Breckinridge, gained a signal victory. Federal loss 730 killed and wounded. Confederate loss 42 killed and 173 wounded.

August 5-8. Guerilla fighting near Stockton, Mo. The Federals claimed a victory. Confederate loss 90 killed and wounded. Federal loss 85 killed and wounded.

August 6. Fight at Pack's Ferry, Western Virginia. Gen. Loring repulsed a large force of Federals.

August 6. The great ram and gunboat "Arkansas" destroyed and abandoned by her officers. The machinery of the boat became disabled, which compelled the crew to destroy the boat to prevent her falling into Federal hands.

August 6th. The notorious Federal General McCook was killed by Partisan Rangers in Tennessee.

August 7. Skirmish near Decatur, Ala. Capt. Roddy defeats a force of Federals, killing several and capturing 123 prisoners. Confederate loss 2 killed and 7 wounded.

August 8th. Fight near Culpepper court-house, Va. The Federals were badly routed, 5 killed and 19 wounded, and 21 taken prisoners.

August 8. Lincoln issues a proclamation calling for 600,000 more men to put down the rebellion.

August 8-9. Battle of South West Mountain, or Cedar Run, Va. The Confederates, under General Jackson, defeated the combined divisions of the Federal army under Banks, McDowell and Seigel. Confederate loss 220 killed and 670 wounded. Gen. Winder killed. Federal loss 300 killed and 900 wounded, and 400 taken prisoners.

August 11. Battle of Independence, Mo. The Confederate Partisans under Col. Hughes and Quantrell, defeated the Federals, killing 29.

August 11. Skirmish at Friar's Point, Miss. The Yankees defeated and put to route, several taken prisoners.

August 15-16. Battle at Lone Jack, Mo. Col. Tracy, the Partisan leader, gained a great victory over the Federals, putting them to route with a loss of 300 killed and wounded. Confederate loss, 73 killed and wounded. Previous to this battle, Colonel Tracy had defeated the enemy in Greenfield, Osceola and Harmonsville, Mo, causing great havoc among the Yankees, capturing large amounts of Federal stores, and took 300 prisoners, and killing over 100 of the enemy.

August 16. A party of Confederates were defeated near Mammoth Cave, Ky.

August 16–17. Skirmish at Bayou Sara, La. The Federals destroyed part of the town—several persons killed.

August 17. Skirmish at Loudon, Ky. The "Kirby Smith Brigade" of cavalry, under Col. Scott, routed the Federals and drove them from the place, capturing 120 men; Confederate loss two killed.

August 18. Barboursville, Ky., taken by the Confederates; 45 Yankees taken prisoners.

August 19 Gen Lee crossed the Rapidan in pursuit of the retreating Federal army under Gen Pope.

August 20 Fight near Union Mills, Buchanan county, Mo; Federals defeated, with a loss of 5 killed and 4 wounded.

August 20 Fort Donelson, Tenn, taken by the Confederates, 1100 Federals taken prisoners.

August 20–21 Fighting near Gallatin, Tenn The Confederates under Gen Morgan defeats and routes the Yankees under Gen Johnson Federal loss 200 killed and wounded, and 500 taken prisoners; Confederate loss 27 killed and 39 wounded.

August 22 Battle of Big Hill, near Richmond, Ky Colonel Scott defeats the Federals. putting them to route with a loss of 23 killed and 65 wounded.

August 22. Skirmish at Warrenton, Va Federals defeated with great loss.

August 22 Gen Stuart surprises the Yankees at Catlett Station, Va, routing the enemy and capturing a large amount of Federal stores, and took 350 prisoners; Confederate loss 2 killed and 5 wounded.

August 26 Skirmishing at Rienzi, Miss A Confederate party made a dash into the Federal camps, capturing 17 prisoners.

August 27 The Federals evacuate Huntsville, Ala

August 26 Fighting near Danville, Ky Our forces defeated and 40 taken prisoners

August 26 Our forces capture the Yankee camps and stores at Manassas Junction.

August 27 Fighting near Bridgeport, Tenn Gen Armstrong defeated the Federals after a sharp fight. Federal loss 70 killed and wounded and 213 taken prisoners.

August 29-30. Skirmish near Bolivar, Tenn. Federals routed with a loss of 90 killed and wounded, and 70 taken prisoners. Confederates 85 killed and wounded.

August 28. Fight at Thoroughfare Gap, Va. The Federals severely defeated, and driven from their strong entrenchments.

August 29-30. Battle of Mt. Zion, or Richmond, Ky. Gen. Kirby Smith achieved a signal victory over the Federals in two hard-fought battles. Federal loss 178 killed and 450 wounded, and 4300 taken prisoners. Confederate loss 125 killed and 300 wounded.

August 29-30. Second Battle on Manassas Plains, Va. Gen. Lee won a glorious victory over the Federal army, under Gen. Pope. Confederate loss 1800 killed and 4,000 wounded. Federal loss 15,000 killed and wounded, and 7,000 taken prisoners.

August 31. Fight at Stevenson, Tenn. The Federals were defeated and compelled to evacuate their strong fortifications.

August 30-Sept. 2d. Col. Jenkins defeated the Federals in several fights in the Kanawha Valley, capturing several prisoners, Federal stores, &c.

September 1st. Battle near Centreville, Va. Federals again defeated by Gen. Jackson. Confederate loss, 45 killed and 135 wounded. The Federal General Kearney killed.

September 1. Skirmish near Germantown, Va. Federals routed.

September 2. Bombardment of Natchez, Miss. A party of Federals landed at Natchez, and were driven back to their gun-boats. The boats then shelled the city for several hours. Two persons were killed in the city.

September 3d. Col. Scott takes possession at Frankfort, Ky., and captures several Yankees.

September 7-10. Guerilla fighting near Salt River, Ky. Federals routed.

September 9. The Confederate Army under Generals Lee and Jackson enters Maryland.

September 9-10. Col. Jenkins defeats the Federals at Buchanan and Ravenswood, Western, Va., capturing large amounts of Federal stores.

September 9th. The Yankee garrison at Williamsburg, Va. was surprised and captured by the Confederates. Federal loss 15 killed and 70 taken prisoners. Confederate loss 17 killed and wounded.

September 9. Fight at Williamsburg, Va. The Federals defeated and driven from the town, with a loss of 18 killed. Confederate loss 3 killed and 5 wounded.

September 9. Washington, North Carolina taken by the Confederates;. the Federals re-captured the place after a hard fight.

September 10. Skirmishing near Helena, Arkansas. Federals defeated.

September 11. Great excitement was created in the country by the report of the capture of Cincinnati.

September 11. Engagement on the St. Johns River, Florida. Federal gunboats repulsed. Our loss two killed and five wounded.

September 13–14. Battle of Cotton Hill, Western Va. Gen. Loring defeats the Federals, capturing all their fortifications, stores, &c. Federal loss 400 killed and wounded. Our loss 25 killed and wounded.

Sept. 15. Fighting at Charleston, Western, Va. Gen. Loring again defeats the Yankees, driving them from the town.

Sept. 14. Battle of Fort Craig, opposite Mumfordsville, Ky., Gen. Chalmers attacked the Federals, after a day's hard fighting, our forces were compelled to fall back with severe loss. General Chalmers is much to be censured for his unnecessary attack and sacrifice of lives. Our loss 65 killed and 275 wounded. Federal loss 18 killed and 30 wounded.

September 13--14. Skirmishing near Opelousas, La. Several fights occurred between Confederate partisans and marauding parties of Yankees. 150 Yankees were captured in one skirmish. The Confederates lost 15 men killed and 13 wounded, and fifty captured in different conflicts.

September 13, 14, 15. Seige and capture of Harper's Ferry, Va. Gen Stonewall Jackson captures the Yankee garrison after three days' hard fighting. 11,583 Yankees were taken prisoners. Our loss 31 killed and 40 wounded. Yankee loss 200 killed and wounded. An immense amount of Federal stores, guns, &c. were taken.

Sept 14. Battle of Boonsboro Gap or South Mountain, Maryland. The Confederates under D. H. Hill fought a most desperate battle, repulsing the Federals and holding possession of the Pass against the enemy who outnumbered them five to one. Federal loss 5,000 killed and wounded. Confederate loss 600 killed and 1,800 wounded.

Sept. 14. Confederate Debt. Up to the first of August, 1862, our debt was $328,748,830.70; and for outstanding requisitions, $18,524,128.15. Receipts at the Treasury, grand total, $302,555,-196.60. Funds to be raised by January 1, 1863, $209,550,487.06; most of which is to be raised by Treasury Notes.

Sept. 13, 14. General Armstrong surprises the Federals at Iuka, Miss., and routes the garrison. Gen. Price enters the town on the 15th, and captures a large amount of Federal stores, &c. Confederate loss 5 killed and wounded. Federal loss 10 killed, 21 wounded.

Sept. 13. Fight at Newtonia, Mo. Federals defeated with a loss of 150 killed and wounded, and 100 taken prisoners.

Sept. 15. Fight at Ponchatoula, La. Federals routed after a brisk engagement. Yankee loss 5 killed and 6 wounded. Confederate loss 2 killed.

Sept. 17. The Federal garrison at Mumfordsville surrendered to Gen. Buckner. 4,800 Yankees taken prisoners.

Sept. 17. The Federals evacuates Cumberland Gap, Tenn.

September 17. Battle of Sharpsburg or Antietam, Maryland. A signal victory was won by the Confederates under Gen. Lee. The Federals under command of Gen. McClellan numbered 90,000 men. The Confederate force amounted to 56,000 men. The Confederates held possession of the battle-field for 24 hours after the fight, and made a successful retreat. Confederate loss, 1,900 killed and 6,915 wounded and 800 taken prisoners. Federal loss, 2,010 killed and 9,416 wounded and 1,044 taken prisoners.

September 18. Fight near Jacksonville, Fla. Federal gun boats repulsed,

September 19. Gen. Lee retreats across the Potomac from Maryland.

September 19–20. Battle of Iuka, Miss. Gen. Price defeated the Federals in the first day's fight, driving them from their fortifications. The second day's battle resulted in the complete rout of the Confederates, with a loss of 265 killed and 687 wounded. Federal loss, 188 killed and 582 wounded.

September 20. Battle of Sheppardstown Ford, Maryland. Gen. A. P. Hill achieved a fine victory over the Federals, repulsing and driving them back across the Potomac with great loss. Confederate loss, 250 killed and wounded. Federal loss, 3,500 killed and wounded.

Sept 21. Mumfordsville, Ky., evacuated by the Confederates,

September 22. Lincoln issues a proclamation declaring all negroes in the Rebel States free after the 1st of January, 1863.

September 26. Gen. Beauregard takes command of the army at Charleston S: C.

September 27. Sabine city taken by the Federals.

September 29. Fight near New Haven, Ky. Confederates defeated. Col. Crawford and 290 Confederates taken prisoners.

October 1. Skirmishing near Middleton, Ky. Federal loss, 11 killed and 19 wounded. Confederate loss, 7 killed and 13 wounded.... Skirmish at Fern Creek, Ky. Federals repulsed with a loss of 7 killed and wounded.... A report was presented to the Confederate Senate, showing the whole number of sick and wounded soldiers admitted into the Hospitals in and around Richmond, since their organization, to the present time, was 99,505, of whom 9,774 have been furloughed, and 7,603 have died.

October 2. Fight near Franklin. N. C. Federals defeated, with a loss of 20 killed and 18 wounded and 40 prisoners.

October 3–4–5. Battle at Corinth, Miss. Confederates won signal victories on the first and second day's fighting; on the third day they lost the battle and were compelled to retreat. Confederate loss, 800 killed and 2,300 wounded, and 388 taken prisoners. Federal loss, 500 killed and 1,800 wounded and 320 taken prisoners.

October 3. Skirmish at Olive Hill, Ky. General Morgan defeats the Home Guards.

October 5. The Confederates make an attack on a fleet of Federal steamboats near Donaldsonville, La., killing several Yankees on board of the steamers.

October 6. Skirmish near Big Burch Mountain, Western Va., several Yankees taken prisoners.

October 7. A party of Confederates under Gen Anderson were surprised and captured at Lavernge, Tenn.

October 8. Battle of Perryville or Chaplin Hill, Ky. A decided victory was gained by the Confederates under Gens. Polk and Hardee, over the Federals. Federal loss 4,000 killed and wounded and 2,000 taken prisoners. Confederate loss 2,700 killed and wounded.

October 9. The city of Galveston, Texas, occupied by the Federals ... Skirmish at Middleburg, Va. Federals defeated. .... Cavalry skirmish near Chaplin Hill, Ky. The Confederates under Col. Scott defeated, with a loss of 9 killed and 5 wounded. Federal loss 5 killed and 11 wounded.... Fight near Frankfort, Ky. Confederates suffered a defeat by the Federals under Dumont. Confederate loss, 4 killed and 75 taken prisoners. Federal loss 5 killed.

October 10–11. Gen. J. E. B. Stuart, with a force of 2,000 men, makes a successful reconnoisance through Pennsylvania, destroying large amounts of Federal property and causing a great panic among the Yankees. During this expedition Gen. Stuart made one of the most extraordinary marches on record, marching 96 miles in 24 hours.... Fight at Augusta, Ky. A party of Confederates after surrendering were fired upon by the Yankees. Lt. Col. Prentice was killed. The Yankees were afterwards attacked in force and a large number killed.

October 17. Fight in Harlan co., Ky. The Confederates attacked and defeated a large party of Union men, killing 4 and 20 taken prisoners....Guerilla fighting near Island 10, Tenn. Confederates defeated with a loss of 5 killed and 11 wounded. Federal loss, 3 killed and 7 wounded.

October 18. Skirmish near Thoroughfare Gap, Va. Confederates repulsed....Murder of Confederates. Ten Confederate prisoners were shot dead by the order of the Federal General, McNeil, at Palmyra, Mo., on account of a raid which the Confederates had made into the town.

October 18–20. Gen. Bragg's army reaches Knoxville, Tenn., on retreat from Ky.

October 18. Skirmish at Lexington, Ky. Morgan's cavalry makes another successful dash into the city, routing the Federals, killing 8 and capturing 150.

October 20. Fighting at Pittman's Ferrry, Ark. A party of Confederate Partisans were attacked and defeated by a large force of the Federal army.

October 21. Skirmishing near Nashville, Tenn. Federals defeated and driven into the city.

October 22. Fight at Pocotaligo and Coosahatchie, S.C. Federals repulsed and driven back. Our loss 22 killed and 50 wounded. Federal loss 15 killed and 100 wounded....Battle at Maysville, Ark. Our forces defeated, with a loss of 52 killed and wounded. Federal loss 7 killed and 19 wounded.

October 23. Skirmish near Waverly, Tenn. Our forces defeated.

October 27. Battle of Albemarle, Bayou Lafourche, La. A desperate fight occurred in which our forces were defeated by a vastly superior force of Federals. Our loss 17 killed, 15 wounded, and 208 taken prisoners. Col. McPheeters of our forces was killed after surrendering to the Yankees....A Confederate camp in Clarkson, Mo., was surprised and routed ; 4 killed and 40 taken prisoners....Skirmish at Snicker's Gap, Va. Federals repulsed and several killed.

October 28. Fight near Fayetteville, Mo. Our forces defeated, with a loss of 5 killed. Federal loss 3 killed and 4 wounded. ....A company of Confederates were surprised and routed with a heavy loss, at Gonzella, Fla.

October 30. Fight at Bollinger's Mills, Ark. Our forces defeated, several taken prisoners.

October 31. Skirmish near Catlett's Station, Va. Federals routed.

November 4. Battle at Williamston. Our forces defeated by a superior force of the Yankees. Our loss, 4 killed and 32 wounded. Federal loss, 7 killed and 28 wounded.

November 5. Skirmishing near Warrenton, Va. Our forces driven from the place, but returned again reinforced, and defeated the Federals, compelling them to retreat. Federal loss, 1 killed and 6 wounded. Our loss none.....Gen. McClellan, of the Yankee army removed by the Government. Gen. Burnside appointed in his place.

November 7. Fight at Haymarket, Va. Major Andrews attacked a large body of Federals, routing them and capturing 30 prisoners, besides taking a large amount of Federal stores.

November 9. The Federals made a raid into Fredericksburg, and were driven from the town, with a loss of 5 killed and wounded. Confederate loss, 1 killed and 3 wounded....A large force of Federals attempted to land at St. Mary's Ga., and were repulsed by the Confederates. The Federals afterwards shelled the town.

November 11. Fight at Castleman's Ferry, Va. Gen. A. P. Hill repulsed a large force of Federals who attempted to cross the river at that point.

November 12. Skirmish near Nashville, Tenn. Gen. Forrest defeated the Abolitionists near Nashville, killing 15 and wounding 37....Fight at Madisonville, Ky. Col. Johnson's cavalry made a dash into the town and scattered the Federals, killing 23 and wounding 100.

November 19. Bombardment of Fort McAllister, Genesis Point, Ga. A heavy bombardment by the Federals was kept up for several hours, when the Yankees retired.

www.ingramcontent.com/pod-product-compliance
Lightning Source LLC
Chambersburg PA
CBHW030411170426
43202CB00010B/1566